OECD
ECONOMIC
SURVEYS

1993-1994

SWITZERLAND

ORGANISATION FOR ECONOMIC CO-OPERATION AND DEVELOPMENT

ORGANISATION FOR ECONOMIC CO-OPERATION AND DEVELOPMENT

Pursuant to Article 1 of the Convention signed in Paris on 14th December 1960, and which came into force on 30th September 1961, the Organisation for Economic Co-operation and Development (OECD) shall promote policies designed:

— to achieve the highest sustainable economic growth and employment and a rising standard of living in Member countries, while maintaining financial stability, and thus to contribute to the development of the world economy;

— to contribute to sound economic expansion in Member as well as non-member countries in the process of economic development; and

— to contribute to the expansion of world trade on a multilateral, non-discriminatory basis in accordance with international obligations.

The original Member countries of the OECD are Austria, Belgium, Canada, Denmark, France, Germany, Greece, Iceland, Ireland, Italy, Luxembourg, the Netherlands, Norway, Portugal, Spain, Sweden, Switzerland, Turkey, the United Kingdom and the United States. The following countries became Members subsequently through accession at the dates indicated hereafter: Japan (28th April 1964), Finland (28th January 1969), Australia (7th June 1971), New Zealand (29th May 1973) and Mexico (18th May 1994). The Commission of the European Communities takes part in the work of the OECD (Article 13 of the OECD Convention).

3 2280 00497 9712

Publié également en français.

Table of contents

Boxes

Tables

Text

Diagrams

Text

BASIC STATISTICS OF SWITZERLAND

THE LAND

Area (1 000 sq. km)	41.3	Major cities, 1992 estimates (1 000 inhabitants):	
Cultivated land, grassland and pastures		Zurich	345.2
(1 000 sq. km), 1979/85	15.8	Basle	175.5
Forest (1 000 sq. km), 1979/85	12.5	Geneva	170.2
		Bern	130.1

THE PEOPLE

Population, December 31, 1992,		Number of foreign workers (1 000),	
estimates (1 000)	6 908	end of August 1993	950.0
Number of persons per sq. km	173	Average increase in the number of	
Net annual rate of population increase		foreign workers census, end of	
(per 1 000 inhabitants, average 1988-91)	9	August (1 000):	
Civilian employment, 1993 (1 000)	3 388	1962-72	16.8
Percentage distribution:		1973-92	4.0
Agriculture	5.6		
Industry and construction	33.2		
Other activities	61.2		

PRODUCTION

Gross domestic product in 1993		Value added by origin in 1990	
(billion Swiss francs)	346.1	(in per cent of GDP at factor cost):	
Growth of real GDP, 1990-93 average		Agriculture	3.1
(annual rate, per cent)	-0.2	Industry	26.3
Real gross fixed investment in 1993		Construction	8.4
(in per cent of GDP)	26.5	Services	62.2
Growth of real investment, 1990-93 average			
(annual rate, per cent)	-3.9		

THE GOVERNMENT[1]

Public consumption in 1993 (in per cent		Composition of Parliament (in per cent):	
of GDP)	14.8		National Council / State Council
Revenue of the Confederation in 1993			
(in per cent of GDP)	9.5		
Total debt in 1993 (in per cent of GDP)	43.7		

	National Council	State Council
Radical Democrats	21.0	39.1
Christian Democrats	18.3	34.8
Socialists	18.5	6.5
Central Democratic Union	11.9	8.7
Other	30.3	10.9
Last elections: 1991		
Next elections: 1995		

FOREIGN TRADE

Exports of goods and services as		Imports of goods and services as	
a percentage of GDP (average 1990-93)	36.0	a percentage of GDP (average 1990-93)	33.4
Commodity exports		Commodity imports	
(fob, million Swiss francs, 1993)	86 659	(cif, million Swiss francs, 1993)	83 767
Percentage distribution:		Percentage distribution:	
By area in 1993		By area in 1993	
To OECD countries	78.2	From OECD countries	91.2
To EEC countries	57.0	From EEC countries	73.6
To OPEC countries	4.0	From OPEC countries	1.2
By categories in 1993		By categories in 1992	
Raw materials and semi-finished goods	28.9	Raw materials and semi-finished goods	30.7
Capital goods	34.7	Energy	4.1
Consumer goods	36.3	Capital goods	25.3
		Consumer goods	39.8

THE CURRENCY

Monetary unit: Swiss franc		Currency unit per US$, average of daily figures:	
		Year 1993	1.4773
		June 1994	1.3742

1. Confederation, cantons and communes.
Note: An international comparison of certain statistics is given in an annex table.

This Survey is based on the Secretariat's study prepared for the annual review of Switzerland by the Economic and Development Review Committee on 24th June 1994.

•

After revisions in the light of discussions during the review, final approval of the Survey for publication was given by the Committee on 11th July 1994.

•

The previous Survey of Switzerland was issued in August 1993.

Introduction

Switzerland's economy had a difficult start into the 1990s: following excessively easy monetary conditions in the late 1980s, inflation accelerated rapidly in 1989 and soon reached unacceptably high rates. The required change in the National Bank's policy stance led to sharply rising interest rates and to exchange-rate appreciation. The economy entered recession at the beginning of 1991, earlier than most European OECD countries. Although the slide in output was rather mild, the downswing lasted longer than the two preceding recessions because the National Bank was constrained by a depreciating Swiss franc in easing its monetary policy at an earlier stage and activity also slowed down in other European economies.

The long-awaited breakthrough on the inflation front occurred during the autumn of 1993, about five years after the National Bank had changed the course of monetary policy towards restriction. In late 1993, inflation dropped precipitously from the long-held level of around 3½ per cent and fell below 1 per cent in the spring of 1994, the upper limit for inflation considered acceptable by the National Bank over the medium term. In late 1993, it also became increasingly clear that activity had passed its trough and was gathering force. These favourable developments are likely to continue in 1994 and 1995.

Improving activity will help to bring actual budget balances under better control, while measures of redressment on all levels of government should reduce the structural components of public deficits. The replacement of the antiquated turnover tax on goods by a modern value-added tax (VAT) as from 1995 – approved by the people in the referendum of November 1993 – will help in this process. It will also eliminate allocative distortions associated with the present turnover tax, which currently imposes – *inter alia* – a sizeable tax burden on investment.

The approval of VAT by the people is an encouraging sign of their recognition of the need for structural reform. Other steps will have to follow to make the economy fit for the challenges ensuing from a rapidly changing international environment. Among them is the completion and implementation of Swisslex (aimed at adapting Swiss legislation to EC law) and the revitalisation project, a comprehensive microeconomic reform package which aims at trimming down impediments to the free working of market forces. Regulations, which usually have been established to attain social objectives but often entail substantial losses in efficiency, will also have to continue to be examined regularly and where necessary, overhauled. This kind of critical examination should include the construction sector, whose relative size is among the biggest in the OECD and whose cyclical responsiveness is particularly high.

Part I of the Survey reviews the salient features of the recent recession and the nascent recovery. The forces which are likely to keep economic activity on an upward trend in the near term are then discussed. Part II first analyses the conduct of monetary policy, while addressing the issue of how much room there is for further monetary relaxation. Recent trends in government finances and their medium-term prospects are then examined, supplemented by a brief analysis of the sustainability of the current fiscal policy setting. Part III provides a progress report on structural reform. Part IV focuses on the analysis of the construction sector, the housing market and land development planning, highlighting the effect of existing regulations and suggesting possible avenues for improved performance. Policy recommendations are given in Part V, together with a summary of the main findings of the analysis.

I. Recent trends and short-term prospects

The end of the recession

Overview

The downturn of the Swiss economy, which started at the beginning of 1991, came to an end in the second quarter of 1993, when domestic demand resumed growth and real GDP stopped falling. In the second half of 1993, output increased by a seasonally-adjusted annual rate (s.a.a.r., hereafter) of 1.0 per cent; output growth accelerated to an annual rate of 2.8 per cent in the first quarter of 1994. Hence, output responded to the easing of monetary policy – measured by changes in M1 and short-term interest rates – after three to four quarters, about the same lag as in the early 1980s.[1] But the recovery was insufficient to compensate for the weakness of the first half-year so that real GDP fell by 0.6 per cent in 1993 as a whole (Table 1). The recorded loss in output was somewhat more pronounced in 1993 than in the first two years of the downturn. In 1992, for example, the contraction in domestic demand was more severe, but its negative impact on output was almost entirely offset by large net exports.

In a nutshell, macroeconomic performance during the past three years can be characterised as follows. In spite of the relatively moderate slowdown in economic activity, the concomitant rise in unemployment and the deterioration of public finances were quite dramatic. The latter, however, partly accounts for the mildness of the recent growth recession, as discretionary fiscal support was lent to the economy in addition to the customary effect of built-in stabilisers. The stabilising effect of the foreign balance on the domestic economy has its counterpart in a record surplus of the current external balance. The shallowness of the downturn meant that disinflation was relatively hesitant (Diagram 1).

Table 1. **Supply and use of resources**

| | 1991 at current prices | | Percentage volume[1] change from previous period, annual rates, s.a. | | | | | | | |
	SF million	Percentage share of GNP	Average 1990-1991	1992	1993	1992 I	1992 II	1993 I	1993 II	1994 Q1
Private consumption	190 490	55.2	1.5	-0.2	-0.8	-0.1	-1.9	-1.7	2.1	4.4
Public consumption	46 640	13.5	3.1	0.5	-0.4	0.5	-1.4	-0.9	1.8	0.3
Gross fixed capital formation	84 810	24.6	0.0	-5.0	-4.3	-5.1	-7.0	-7.0	4.5	1.2
Construction	55 880	16.2	-0.6	-2.3	-4.2	-0.8	-6.3	-5.9	1.6	5.5
Machinery and equipment	28 930	8.4	1.2	-9.6	-4.3	-12.2	-8.2	-9.0	10.2	-6.2
Final domestic demand	321 940	93.2	1.3	-1.4	-1.7	-1.4	-3.2	-3.0	2.7	2.9
Change in stocks[2,3]	4 545	1.3	-0.8	-1.7	0.3	-1.3	0.0	0.4	-0.3	-0.1
Total domestic demand	326 485	94.5	0.9	-3.0	-1.4	-3.8	-3.3	-2.2	2.1	2.6
Exports of goods and services	116 720	33.8	1.1	3.4	0.8	5.3	-0.5	-1.4	6.7	8.0
Imports of goods and services	112 130	32.5	0.6	-3.8	-1.2	-4.2	-5.8	-3.7	9.1	7.1
Change in foreign balance[2]	4 590	1.3	0.4	3.2	0.9	2.1	1.2	0.5	-0.6	0.1
Gross domestic product	331 075	95.9	1.1	-0.1	-0.6	0.0	-0.9	-1.2	1.0	2.8
Gross national product	345 390	100.0	0.5	-0.5						
GDP deflator			5.6	2.6	2.5	2.1	2.4	2.5	2.7	1.9
Private consumption deflator			5.5	4.1	2.9	3.5	4.0	2.7	2.1	-0.9
Index of industrial production[4]			1.6	-0.7	-0.5	0.5	-2.5	-4.7	10.4	7.1

1. At 1980 prices.
2. As a percentage of GDP of the previous period.
3. This item is partly a residual value; it also contains statistical errors.
4. Excluding hydro-electric power and electric and gas utilities.
Source: Département fédéral de l'économie publique, *La vie économique; KOF/ETH, Konjunktur;* OECD.

Diagram 1. **MACROECONOMIC PERFORMANCE**

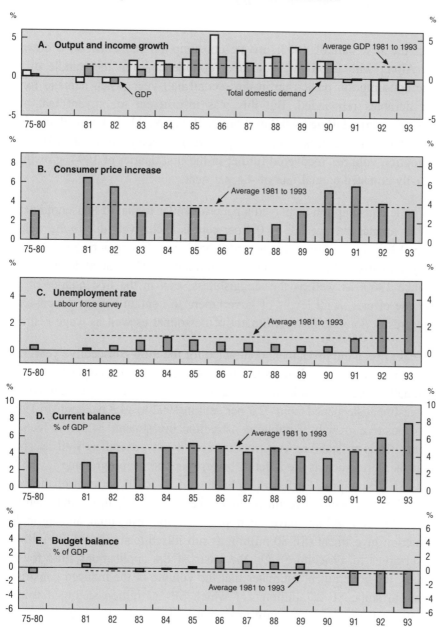

Source: OECD.

Domestic demand turning around

In the first half of 1993, private consumption remained on a downward trend. Along with improving consumer confidence from the middle of 1993, private consumption picked up in the second half-year, when demand for consumer durables rebounded. But this was insufficient to prevent real private consumption from falling by 0.8 per cent in 1993, roughly in line with the decline in real disposable incomes and the steepest yearly decline since 1975. Household consumption volumes recovered further in the first quarter of 1994, growing at a seasonally-adjusted annual rate of 4.4 per cent.

Public consumption displayed a pattern similar to that of household expenditures: its annual average fall by 0.4 per cent is exclusively due to the weakness in early 1993, while it grew by around 2 per cent (s.a.a.r.) during the remainder of the year, partly reflecting the decrease in inflation. The annual decline, the first one since 1960, as well as the sluggishness seen in the first quarter of 1994, mirror the efforts of all levels of government to contain budget deficits, which dictated restrictions on the recruitment of personnel as well as wage restraint.

Real gross fixed investment contracted for the third consecutive year, falling by 4.3 per cent in 1993. But fixed investment recovered vigorously during the second half of the year and kept growing in early 1994. The decrease in construction investment steepened from –2.3 per cent in 1992 to –4.3 per cent[2] in 1993, in spite of positive growth of public construction investment,[3] which reflects government efforts to stabilise construction activity in general as well as specific support measures such as the federal "investment bonus programme". The latter devotes SF 200 million for federal subsidies of 15 to 20 per cent of the cost of additional infrastructure investment undertaken by municipalities and cantons. In addition, SF 100 million have been provided for residential and agricultural construction investment (SF 80 million as subsidised loans and SF 20 million as pure subsidies to agriculture). On the basis of the applications filed for these subsidies, the government estimates that the volume of the induced construction amounts to some SF 2.7 billion[4] (of which SF 1.7 billion stemmed from the "investment bonus"), a presently unknown part of it having become effective already in 1993. The full thrust of the programme will, however, be felt only in 1994.

14

The decline of residential investment (estimated at $-\frac{1}{2}$ per cent in 1993) seems to have come to an end, partly reflecting the support offered by subsidised federal housing loans but possibly already the consequence of lower mortgage interest rates and reduced construction costs. KOF estimates are for a decrease in real business construction by more than 10 per cent in 1993, a consequence of the still huge stock of unused structures. Total real construction investment picked up, however, in the fourth quarter of 1993 and the first quarter of 1994.

After a steep fall for nine consecutive quarters, investment in machinery and equipment turned around by the middle of 1993. It picked up by a vigorous 23 per cent (s.a.a.r.) in the fourth quarter, but for 1993 on average it fell for the third consecutive year, by 4.3 per cent. The recorded decline in the first quarter of 1994 (–3.1 per cent, s.a.a.r.) has to be assessed in view of the surge in the preceding quarter. The share of machinery investment in nominal GDP fell from close to 10 per cent in late 1989 to under $7\frac{1}{2}$ per cent, below its average of $8\frac{1}{4}$ per cent over the 1980s.

It is still unclear to what extent lower interest rates contributed to the rise of machinery investment during the second half of 1993.[5] Capacity utilisation in industry bottomed out at 79 per cent in the first quarter of 1993, and has increased since. But at $82\frac{1}{2}$ per cent in the first quarter of 1994, it remained below its long-term average of $84\frac{1}{2}$ per cent. However, after the recession in 1982, machinery and equipment investment picked up when the capacity utilisation rate stood at 80 per cent, and in the mid-1970s, investment already resumed growth when this indicator was at a low 77 to 78 per cent. A plausible hypothesis seems to be that the current high Swiss franc exchange rate forces entrepreneurs to strengthen their competitiveness by stepped-up modernisation of their capital stock, a response observed earlier. In addition, such a strategy has been made attractive by the fall in prices of imported investment goods in 1993 (–1 $\frac{1}{2}$ per cent), due to the franc appreciation and generally depressed demand for investment goods.

Potential output

At the present juncture, the index of capacity utilisation in industry could give a somewhat exaggerated impression of *economically viable* spare capacity. This would be in accordance with the notion that the growth of potential output is less stable than is often assumed,[6] and may change significantly over the economic cycle, reflecting – *inter alia* – the varying growth of the business sector

15

capital stock in response to fluctuations in investment. Although the capital stock tends to react to *changes* in investment with considerable inertia, given that the latter is only the second derivative of the former, the changes in machinery and equipment investment (Diagram 2) and – to a somewhat lesser extent – in business construction over the 1980s were large enough to have a marked impact on productive potential. Estimates of the OECD Secretariat suggest that the growth of the business sector capital stock accelerated from some 2½ per cent in the early 1980s to about 4½ per cent in 1990, which led to estimates for potential output growth of 2½ to 2¾ per cent in the late 1980s. During the recent recession, the growth of the capital stock slowed down, to around 2½ per cent in 1993, which also should have brought down potential output growth, possibly to below 2 per cent at present, the exact magnitude depending on the assumption made for the potential labour force. An alternative approach, using the Hodrick-Prescott filter technique, arrives also at about 2½ per cent potential output growth just before the recent recession and suggests a significant slowdown subsequently, to about 1½ per cent in 1993.

Comparison of the current downturn with past cyclical episodes

With the latest recession being over now, it may be of interest to compare briefly some of its main features with those of previous cyclical downturns. What appears most striking is that the recent recession was much less steep than the slump in the mid-1970s and less pronounced than the recession of 1982, but that with a length of about 10 quarters it lasted longer than any other period of slack during the past 40 years. Given that tighter monetary policies are usually run in the beginning of a recession, it appears plausible to view the severity and length of a stabilisation exercise as inversely related: in the latest episode, the process of disinflation was slow because of the relatively shallow downturn in activity so that the recession had to last commensurably longer to break inflation expectations and to get inflation out of the economic system.

The major factor which prolonged the recent process of stabilisation was that, in contrast to earlier episodes, help from exchange rate appreciation came later than usual (Diagram 3), so that this time more weight had to be placed on the transmission of monetary impulses through domestic channels. Although the concomitant loss in output was not higher than in previous stabilisation exercises, the consequences in terms of foregone employment were more painful than in the

Diagram 2. **OUTPUT AND INVESTMENT: AN INTERNATIONAL COMPARISON**

Index 1980 S1 = 100

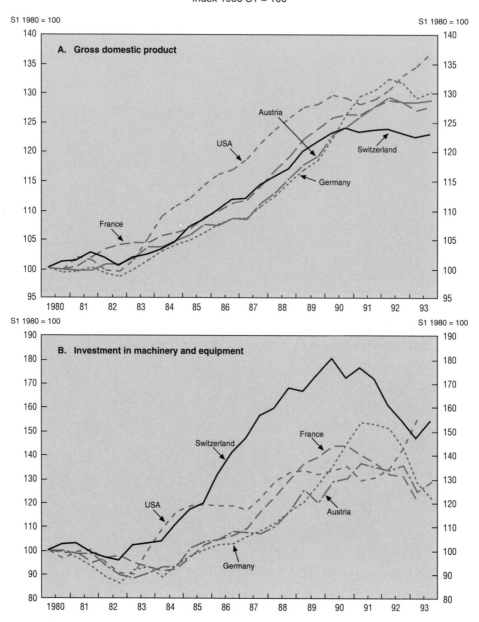

Source: OECD.

17

Diagram 3. **THE RESPONSE OF INFLATION TO MONETARY STABILISATION**

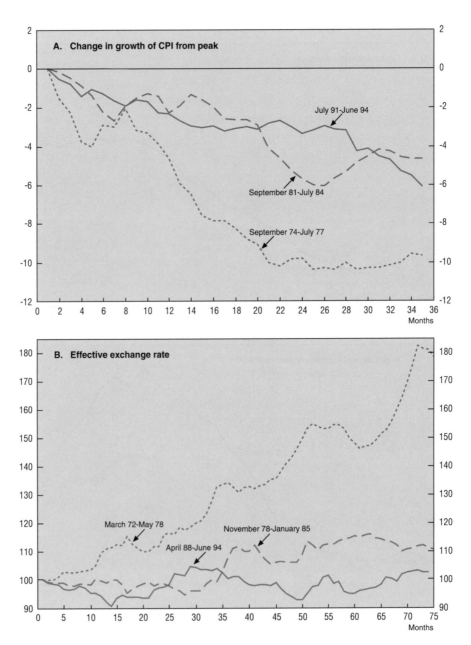

Source: OECD.

1982 recession (Table 2). In relation to the magnitude of the stabilisation task, the relative employment cost of disinflation in the most recent episode was as high as that in the deep crisis of the mid-1970s.

When comparing major demand components during different periods of economic slump, the stabilising effect of exports during the recent recession stands out (Diagram 4). The relative strength of export demand is consistent with the observation that during most of the recent period of disinflation the Swiss franc appreciated by less than during earlier episodes of monetary tightness. Moreover, the fact that the Swiss recession set in earlier than in most other European OECD countries explains in part why Swiss export markets kept on growing during the first two years of downturn; support also came from strong demand from non-OECD countries. Another stabilising factor during the first two years of the downswing was the relative steadiness of household consumption, which compares favourably with earlier episodes of decline: private consumption bolstered demand in 1991 even though employment was shrinking, while it fell right at the beginning of the previous two recession periods.[7]

Table 2. **The costs of disinflation**

Recession period	1975/76		1982		1991/93	
	Absolute	Relative[2]	Absolute	Relative[2]	Absolute	Relative[2]
Cumulative fall in real GDP[1]	7.6	0.8	0.9	0.2	0.7	0.1
Cumulative deviation of real GDP from Hodrick-Prescott trend	9.1	0.9	3.1	0.5	3.5	0.6[4]
Cumulative fall in total employment[1]	7.7	0.8	0.0	0.0	5.0	0.8
Cumulative deviation of total employment from Hodrick-Prescott trend	6.7	0.6	1.5	0.3	3.1	0.5[4]

1.   In percentage points.
2.   Absolute value divided by difference between inflation peak and trough.
3.   The inflation rate of 0.4 per cent in May 1994 has been used as the inflation trough.
4.   Includes OECD Secretariat projections which imply that output and employment levels attain their trend values only in 1995.
Source: OECD.

Diagram 4. **THE RECENT RECESSION COMPARED WITH 1975-76 AND 1982**

Indices of seasonally-adjusted data, volumes

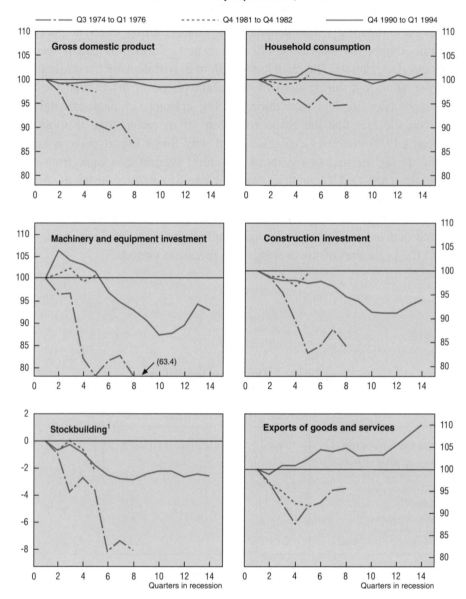

1. Contribution to GDP growth, cumulative over period.
Source: OECD.

Further losses in employment

The loss of jobs, which begun in 1991, continued in 1993: employment dropped by 2.8 per cent, which was much more rapid than the decline in output for the second year in a row (Diagram 5). Another fall in total employment was recorded in the first quarter of 1994 (–4.1 per cent, s.a.a.r.), in spite of the recovery of output. The implied increase in labour productivity was 2¼ per cent in 1993 and 2 per cent in 1992, substantially above the average productivity growth of only 1 per cent during the 1980s and also higher than the long-term average of 1¾ per cent. The stagnation of productivity in 1991 was typical for the early stage of a recession, when the adjustment of employment usually follows the slowdown of production with a lag.

The number of jobs lost from the employment peak in the third quarter of 1990 to the trough three years later amounts to about 192 000, a sizeable 5.4 per cent of peak employment. Each of the three major sectors – industry, construction and services – was affected, with the construction sector hit hardest, losing

Diagram 5. **OUTPUT AND EMPLOYMENT**

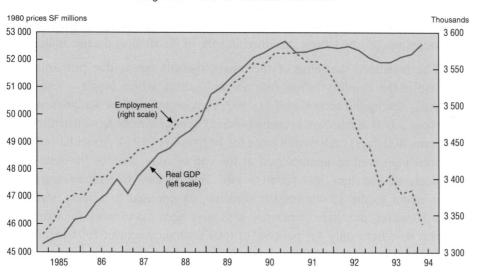

Source: KOF/ETH, *Konjunktur.*

21

6.3 per cent of its jobs in 1993. Once again, the decline in services employment – at 1.6 per cent in 1993 – turned out to be comparatively mild. While actual employment contracted throughout 1993, seasonally-adjusted data suggest some levelling-off of the downturn during the second half of the year. The improvement in late 1993 appears to be most accentuated in the construction sector, which is possibly an early reflection of the pick-up in construction investment towards the end of the year. In contrast, employment in industry continued its steep decline throughout 1993 and in early 1994. Other recent indicators of inproving labour demand are the increase in the number of vacancies in January and February 1994 and the rise in (s.a.) overtime worked in industry during the second half of 1993.

With the labour force declining, but by much less than total employment, the rate of unemployment continued its upward trend throughout 1993; for the year on average, it stood at 4.5 per cent, 2 percentage points higher than in 1992. The seasonally-adjusted unemployment rate appears to have peaked at 5.0 per cent in the fourth quarter of 1993 and declined to 4.8 per cent in the period from March to May 1994, which could be a first indication of a turnaround. This seems to support the view that this time the lag between a recovery of production and an improvement in the labour market may be shorter than experienced earlier. This could be so because enterprises appear to have hoarded less labour during the recent cyclical downturn than previously. Instead, entrepreneurs resorted to rapid and sometimes drastic labour shedding, in spite of the shallow decline in demand.

The registered flattening of the unemployment rate is due primarily to a decrease in the monthly inflow into unemployment, which began – seasonally adjusted – during the second half of 1993. Provisional outflow statistics suggest that about 3 000 unemployed reached federal unemployment benefit termination (now after 400 days) each month since the beginning of 1994. About half of them remained registered as unemployed at the end of May, and, of the remainder, half declared that they had found a job. This appears to indicate a genuine improvement in the labour market situation, as opposed to a mere statistical effect. However, the share of persons who have been out of work for more than one year rose from only 4.4 per cent of total unemployment in 1991 to 25.4 per cent in the first quarter of 1994 (Table 3).

Other indicators of the structure of unemployment display broadly the same pattern, as highlighted in the special labour market chapter of last year's OECD

Table 3. **Level and structure of recent unemployment**

	1990		1991		1992		1993		1994 First quarter	
	Number	Rate [1]	Number	Rate [1]	Number	Rate [1]	Number	Rate [1]	Number	Rate [1]
Total	18 133	0.5	39 222	1.1	92 308	2.5	163 135	4.5	185 895	5.1
According to region										
German speaking	8 365	0.3	18 889	0.7	51 565	2.0	96 959	3.7	109 466	4.2
French and Italian speaking	9 768	1.0	20 333	2.0	40 743	4.0	66 176	6.5	76 429	7.6
According to gender										
Women	8 306	0.6	16 507	1.2	37 591	2.7	66 571	4.7	75 845	5.4
Men	9 827	0.4	22 715	1.0	54 717	2.5	96 564	4.4	110 050	5.0
According to citizenship										
Swiss	10 525	0.4	22 370	0.8	55 636	2.0	99 631	3.5	111 780	4.0
Foreign	7 608	0.9	16 852	2.1	36 672	4.5	63 504	7.8	74 115	9.1
According to age										
15-24 years	2 887	0.4	7 377	1.1	19 883	3.0	32 098	4.8	32 533	4.9
25-49 years	11 676	0.5	25 613	1.2	58 480	2.7	103 459	4.8	118 642	5.5
50 years and more	3 570	0.5	6 232	0.8	13 945	1.8	27 578	3.5	34 720	4.4
According to sectors										
Agriculture	159	0.1	317	0.2	827	0.4	1 522	0.8	2 024	1.1
Energy, mining	26	0.1	83	0.3	234	0.9	448	1.8	560	2.3
Arts and crafts, industry	4 371	0.5	10 408	1.2	24 623	3.0	40 916	5.1	44 773	5.8
Construction	1 331	0.4	3 510	1.1	9 504	3.0	17 441	5.8	20 747	7.1
Distributive trade, catering, repairs	5 313	0.6	10 604	1.3	24 154	3.0	42 437	5.5	49 336	6.5
Transport and communication	558	0.3	1 288	0.6	3 089	1.4	5 183	2.4	5 845	2.8
Banking, insurance, consultancy	2 452	0.6	6 068	1.4	13 370	3.1	20 970	4.9	22 605	5.3
Other services	2 866	0.6	4 986	0.9	11 624	2.2	18 827	3.6	22 035	4.2
Government	523	0.4	918	0.7	2 321	1.7	3 784	2.8	4 428	3.3
Not specified [2]	534	–	1 042	–	2 562	–	11 607	–	13 542	–
Total	18 133	0.5	39 222	1.1	92 308	2.6	163 135	4.8	185 895	5.6

	Share in %	Share in %	Share in %	Share in %	Share in %
According to duration					
0-6 months	13 860 76.4	30 245 77.1	60 633 65.7	85 346 52.3	85 628 46.1
7-12 months	3 085 17.0	7 255 18.5	23 636 25.6	48 939 30.0	53 030 28.5
More than 1 year	1 188 6.6	1 722 4.4	8 039 8.7	28 850 17.7	47 237 25.4
According to function					
Specialists	8 038 44.3	17 147 43.7	43 764 47.4	80 132 49.1	91 355 49.1
Auxiliaries	8 625 47.6	18 761 47.8	39 170 42.4	64 327 39.4	72 080 38.8
Apprentices/students	443 2.4	1 173 3.0	4 449 4.8	9 936 6.1	12 294 6.6
Other	1 027 5.7	2 141 5.5	4 925 5.4	8 740 5.4	10 166 5.5

1. Official unemployment statistics include those who are partially unemployed. With the exception of sectoral unemployment rates, official unemployment rates are expressed as a percentage of the work-force in the 1990 population census; sectoral unemployment rates are expressed as a percentage of the work-force in the corresponding period.
2. Persons seeking employment for the first time or re-entering the work-force.
Source: Office fédéral de l'industrie, des arts et métiers et du travail (unemployment), Office fédéral de la statistique (employment).

Survey of Switzerland. In particular, unemployment of young persons aged 15 to 24 years, which rose somewhat faster than total joblessness during the recent recession, remained not only low by international comparison but is also characterised by a shorter duration than that of higher age groups.[8]

Breakthrough on the inflation front

From its peak rate of 6.6 per cent at the middle of 1991, Swiss consumer price inflation was brought down to about 3½ per cent after about one year, but then it hovered around this rate for as long as 15 months until October 1993 (Diagram 6). Sticky service prices – notably rents, but also the lagged adjustment of administered prices to higher costs – account for most of the stubbornness of inflation witnessed during this period. Another temporary inflation push came from the increase in the customs duty on gasoline by SF 0.20 per litre in March 1993, which may have added ½ percentage point to average consumer price inflation in 1993.

Diagram 6. **CONSUMER PRICE INFLATION AND SELECTED COMPONENTS**
Year-on-year change

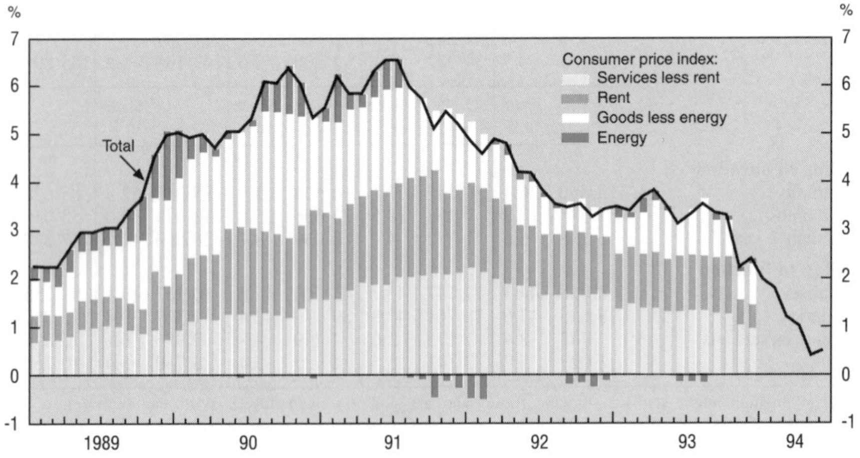

Note: The decomposition is not possible for 1994 due to a change in definitions.
Source: OECD, *Main Economic Indicators.*

24

The twelve-month rise in the CPI eventually dropped to 2.2 per cent in November 1993, when decreasing mortgage interest rates induced a marked deceleration of housing rent increases[9] to 2.3 per cent, from a 5.9 per cent rate in October. For 1993 on average, consumer price inflation still stood at a comparatively high 3.3 per cent, 0.5 percentage point above average inflation in the OECD (excluding Turkey).

During the early months of 1994, CPI inflation fell further, to 0.4 per cent in May and 0.5 per cent in June. Hence, about 5½ years after the swing in the stance of monetary policy towards restriction, the twelve-month inflation rate reached the National Bank's implicit objective of 0 to 1 per cent. Switzerland has accordingly brought its inflation rate distinctly below the OECD average (Diagram 7). The recent drop in the twelve-month rate is largely due to the effect of last year's petrol tax increase falling out of the calculation. But weak world oil prices and the damping effect of the Swiss franc appreciation on import prices also helped. With the gap between actual and potential output remaining sizeable, further consumer price disinflation is to be expected in the coming months.

Diagram 7. **INTERNATIONAL COMPARISON OF CONSUMER PRICES**
Percentage change over corresponding period of previous year

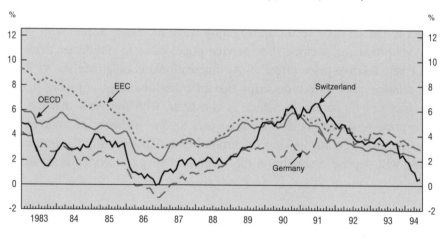

1. Excluding Turkey.
Source: OECD, *Main Economic Indicators.*

However, underlying inflation, as measured by the GDP deflator, still stood at around 2½ per cent throughout 1993 and in early 1994. This suggests that keeping inflation within the National Bank's preferred range of 0 to 1 per cent will be a difficult task.

Price stability has already been achieved for three full years at the level of the wholesale price index[10] or supply price index, which includes only goods (Table 4). Supply prices of home produced goods have been rising rather moderately – below 1 per cent since the beginning of 1992 – while prices of imported goods have even been falling since the second quarter of 1990. The price damping impact of imported goods and services, largely attributable to the appreciating Swiss franc, but also to generally low inflation abroad, is visible at the consumer level as well, although in a somewhat less pronounced manner. Among the primarily home-produced consumer goods and services, the inflationary effect of service prices – rents in particular – stands out and appears crucial for future price performance. This is the more so as help from an ever appreciating Swiss franc appears neither realistic nor desirable.

Part of the service price stickiness is attributable to the fact that, as is also the case in other countries, many services are protected from foreign competition. Another reason is typically lower measured productivity gains in the production of services, although there are services where the potential for productivity increases is high (for example, banking and real estate). But in general, if workers in the services sector are to enjoy wage increases in line with those in the goods-producing sectors, then service prices have to rise faster than goods prices (the "relative price effect"). An international comparison shows that the Swiss relative price effect outstrips that of other countries enjoying high *per capita* incomes (Diagram 8), which is consistent with the view that the Swiss service price resilience is due in large part to low intensity of competition.[11] Hence, the prospects for locking in current low inflation during the forthcoming upswing will depend crucially on the success in keeping service price inflation at bay.

The process of disinflation was supported from the labour cost side. Official statistics are for an average increase in wage rates of 2.6 per cent in 1993, after 4.7 per cent in 1992. The implied fall in the real "consumption wage" by 0.7 per cent in 1993 is ascribable to the deteriorating labour market. Compared with the

Table 4. Price trends

Percentage changes from previous year

	Weight in %	1989	1990	1991	1992	1993	1991				1992				1993				1994
							Q1	Q2	Q3	Q4	Q1	Q2	Q3	Q4	Q1	Q2	Q3	Q4	Q1
Wholesale price index (1963 weights)[1]	100.0	4.3	1.5	0.4	0.1	0.2	0.5	0.2	0.2	0.7	0.3	0.5	-0.2	-0.1	0.4	0.0	0.5	-0.1	-0.7
Raw materials and semi-manufactured products	61.4	5.4	0.0	-0.7	-0.4		-1.2	-1.0	-0.6	0.0	-0.3	-0.6	-0.7	-0.1	-0.4				
Energy and related products	9.0	6.0	3.3	1.4	-0.2		4.4	4.3	-1.1	-1.7	-2.1	1.6	-0.2	-0.2	3.5				
Consumer goods	29.6	1.7	3.5	2.1	1.2		2.2	1.0	2.2	2.9	2.2	1.9	0.6	-0.1	0.6				
Home produced goods	70.6	3.2	2.3	1.3	0.7	0.4	1.5	1.0	1.2	1.5	0.9	0.9	0.5	0.7	0.9	0.5	0.6	-0.3	-0.6
Imported goods	29.4	7.5	-0.9	-2.1	-1.7	-0.3	-2.3	-2.1	-2.5	-1.4	-1.3	-0.7	-2.2	-2.6	-1.1	-1.2	0.3	0.7	-1.0
Consumer price index[2]	100.0	3.2	5.4	5.9	4.0	3.3	5.9	6.2	6.1	5.3	4.8	4.4	3.6	3.4	3.5	3.5	3.5	2.7	1.7
Goods	50.8	2.5	4.5	3.5	1.1	1.7	4.1	4.1	3.3	2.4	1.5	1.6	0.8	0.6	1.4	1.8	1.9	1.6	0.7
Non-durables	42.6	2.7	4.9	3.8	0.9	1.4	4.5	4.4	3.5	2.5	1.3	1.4	0.5	0.2	1.2	1.4	1.8	1.7	0.8
of which:																			
Food	21.0	1.7	5.4	4.5	0.9	0.0	4.8	4.5	4.4	4.5	2.2	1.2	0.2	0.0	0.2	-0.4	0.1	0.2	0.1
Heating and lighting[3]	5.0	10.7	7.5	3.1	-2.6	1.2	9.5	8.4	2.3	-6.0	-7.2	2.0	-1.1	-3.6	2.8	0.8	0.8	0.4	-3.7
Services	49.2	3.7	6.2	8.0	6.5	4.6	7.4	8.2	8.5	7.8	7.6	6.7	6.0	5.8	5.2	4.9	4.7	3.6	2.5
of which:																			
Rents	18.0	3.7	8.6	9.9	6.9	5.1	9.6	10.3	10.7	9.2	8.5	7.0	6.3	6.0	5.8	5.6	5.7	3.4	2.9
Home produced goods and services	70.4	3.0	5.8	6.8	5.0	3.6	6.6	6.9	7.1	6.6	6.0	5.2	4.6	4.4	4.1	3.8	3.8	2.9	2.1
Imported goods and services	29.6	3.7	4.4	3.2	1.1	2.2	3.9	4.3	3.0	1.5	1.3	1.9	0.8	0.4	1.7	2.5	2.6	2.1	0.6
Export prices[4]	7.4	1.1	2.1	1.5	1.2	1.2	-0.3	1.4	3.6	4.0	3.4	2.4	0.0	0.3	2.0	2.6	0.2	0.3	-0.9
Import prices[4]	9.0	-0.8	0.6	1.9	1.9	-1.0	-2.5	0.6	3.2	1.0	2.7	3.7	0.5	0.8	0.0	-1.4	-1.0	-1.4	-6.4

1. From May 1993: Total supply price index (= Total of producer and import price indices).
2. December 1982 = 100; May 1993 = 100 as from the second quarter 1993.
3. Until the first quarter of 1993 "heating and lighting"; thereafter, "energy".
4. Change in the price deflator of goods and services, national accounts basis; break in series in 1988.
Source: Département fédéral de l'économie publique, La vie économique.

Diagram 8. **THE RISE IN RELATIVE SERVICE PRICES**[1]

1985 = 100

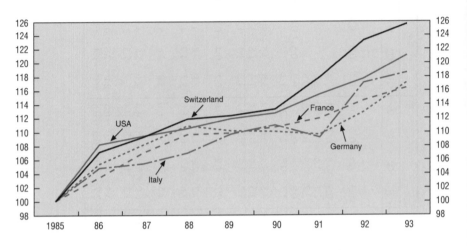

1. Index of consumer prices for services divided by index of consumer prices for goods.
Source: OECD.

Diagram 9. **LABOUR COST AND PRODUCTIVITY**

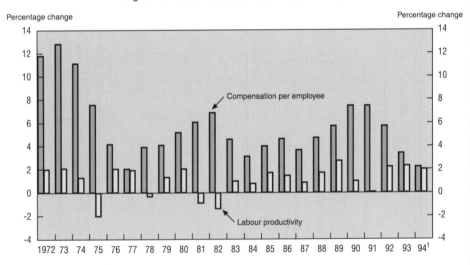

1. Projection.
Source: OECD.

steep fall in employment and the dramatic rise in unemployment, the decline in real wages appears comparatively small. This seems even more so when wages are deflated by the GDP deflator, which may be more relevant for companies; the so-defined "real production wage" remained unchanged in 1993.[12]

Wage settlements for 1994 are estimated to lead to nominal wage increases of about 1³/₄ per cent, hence on average more than 1¹/₂ percentage points below the twelve-month rate of price inflation of 3.4 per cent in October 1993.[13] This has to be assessed against the background of another sizeable loss in employment and a further jump in the unemployment rate by 1.8 percentage points to 4.8 per cent during the twelve months to October 1993. On the basis of Secretariat projections, the degree of wage moderation achieved in combination with further productivity gains will result in virtually stagnant unit labour costs and will lend further support to disinflation from the cost side (Diagram 9).

A record current external surplus

Supported by strong market growth, the preceding real exchange-rate depreciation and the preparedness of exporters to accept lower profit margins, exports of goods and services proved the main engine of domestic activity in 1992. However, the Swiss franc began to appreciate in both nominal and real terms from May 1992 until the spring of 1994 – with an interruption in the winter of 1992/93 – while the growth of Swiss export markets slowed down in the second half of 1992 and even turned negative in the first half of 1993. As a result, export growth lost its momentum in late 1992 and in the first half of 1993. With the recovery of export markets from the second half of 1993 onward the volume of merchandise exports resumed growth, in spite of losses in price competitiveness. For the average of 1993, merchandise export volumes grew by a modest 0.6 per cent, which is nevertheless quite remarkable against the background of falling demand in trading partner countries; it compares favourably with the export performance of other OECD countries (Diagram 10). The growth of merchandise export volumes quickened in the first quarter of 1994 to the twelve-monthly growth rate of 5.8 per cent. But given the very strong Swiss franc, some deterioration in *relative* export performance is likely in 1994. This is corroborated by the declining trend of seasonally-adjusted merchandise export volumes during the first five months of 1994.

Diagram 10. **COMPETITIVENESS AND TRADE**[1]

Index 1987 = 100

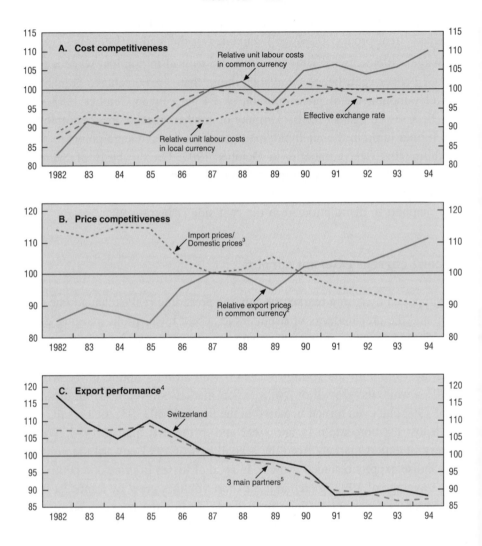

1. 1993 and 1994 figures are Secretariat projections.
2. Manufactures.
3. Import prices of total goods and services divided by deflator of total domestic demand.
4. Ratio between export volumes of manufactures and export markets for manufactures.
5. Germany, France and Italy.
Source: OECD.

Investment goods, which account for more than 37 per cent of total exports, remain the dominant commodity category of Swiss exports. With subdued machinery and equipment investment in important partner countries, real investment goods exports fell 2.2 per cent in 1993, despite price cuts of some 1 per cent (Table 5). However, an improvement in both sales volumes and profit margins was achieved towards the end of 1993 and in the first quarter of 1994. Exports of raw materials and semi-finished goods developed much in parallel to investment goods exports. Consumer goods exports, however, stood out, growing by 5.6 per cent in real terms in 1993, markedly faster than real private consumption in the OECD area. Exports of consumer goods displayed a trend deterioration at the end of 1993 and during the first five months of 1994.

Exports (in current prices) to the OECD area as a whole as well as to European OECD countries declined in 1993, by 1.5 and 2.2 per cent, respectively, which suggests market share losses. Exports to individual OECD countries reflect to a large measure the prevailing phase of the business cycle in these economies. However, the small fall in exports to Germany (by 1.2 per cent) in 1993 when German imports were declining steeply reveals a remarkable export performance in Switzerland's biggest single country market (absorbing about one-quarter of Swiss merchandise exports). The strength of exports to the United Kingdom and to Ireland stands out and is striking given the Swiss franc's appreciation against these countries' currencies. On the other hand, the steep decline in deliveries to Italy, which exceeds the contraction in its domestic demand by a large margin, seems attributable to the sizeable depreciation of the Italian lira against the franc. The weakness of exports to OECD countries was largely compensated for by the growth of sales to non-OECD countries – now more than one-fifth of Swiss export markets – by 8.7 per cent in 1993 (Diagram 11). Although starting from a relatively low level, the increase of exports to China and Singapore (by around 50 per cent each) and to the Newly Independent States of the former Soviet Union (nearly 30 per cent) in 1993 is a remarkable achievement. The first quarter of 1994 saw a recovery of Swiss sales to the OECD area and further strengthening of exports to non-OECD economies (a fall in exports to China was more than offset by vigorous sales growth to South Korea).

Notwithstanding their growing attractiveness as a result of falling relative prices, import volumes largely followed the cyclical movement of domestic

Table 5. Foreign trade by commodity group[1]

| | | 1991 values | | | | Percentage change from same period in previous year | | | | | | | | |
		SF million	% share	1992	1993	1992 Q1	1992 Q2	1992 Q3	1992 Q4	1993 Q1	1993 Q2	1993 Q3	1993 Q4	1994 Q1
Imports, cif, total	Volume	88 681	100.0	-4.3	-1.2	-0.2	-5.2	-4.8	-6.4	-7.6	-3.1	-0.1	5.1	9.4
	Price			2.2	-2.2	4.2	4.2	0.6	-0.7	-1.4	-2.5	-1.4	-2.0	-6.5
Raw materials and semi-finished goods	Volume	26 914	30.3	-1.4	-1.3	-1.6	-3.5	1.6	-1.3	-5.8	-1.5	-1.4	2.9	10.5
	Price			1.0	-2.7	1.7	3.1	-0.1	-1.4	-1.2	-3.2	-2.8	-2.7	-5.9
Fuels	Volume	4 359	4.9	1.2	-8.5	16.2	4.7	-0.9	-12.6	-9.7	-13.7	-14.2	5.0	-1.3
	Price			-11.7	-3.5	-15.7	-4.0	-12.2	-14.8	-0.7	-3.9	-2.1	-7.1	-17.8
Investment goods	Volume	23 983	27.0	-10.3	-4.1	-6.2	-8.3	-14.2	-12.6	-10.6	-11.1	-1.1	6.9	10.2
	Price			4.4	-1.5	8.3	5.6	2.4	1.1	-1.5	-0.2	-0.8	-2.1	-7.2
Consumer goods	Volume	33 425	37.7	-2.9	1.5	3.3	-5.4	-3.4	-5.2	-7.0	2.9	3.4	5.4	9.5
	Price			3.5	-2.1	5.9	5.2	1.7	0.3	-1.6	-3.3	-0.8	-0.8	-5.5
Exports, fob, total	Volume	82 021	100.0	4.3	0.6	7.1	3.7	5.5	0.2	-2.4	-1.1	0.5	5.0	5.8
	Price			0.7	0.0	2.8	1.5	-0.7	0.3	-0.7	0.8	0.5	-0.2	0.2
Raw materials and semi-finished goods	Volume	24 820	30.3	2.8	-1.7	3.9	1.2	3.9	-0.3	-4.2	-4.3	1.0	2.6	9.8
	Price			0.6	-0.7	3.2	1.2	-0.5	0.8	-0.7	0.3	-1.8	-2.0	-4.4
Investment goods	Volume	30 490	37.2	0.0	-2.2	2.3	0.9	2.0	-4.5	-8.9	-4.6	-1.8	4.5	6.5
	Price			2.0	-1.1	3.9	0.4	1.3	2.4	1.2	0.3	-0.6	-3.3	-1.3
Consumer goods	Volume	26 586	32.4	10.6	5.6	16.1	9.1	11.1	6.1	6.3	5.4	2.2	7.0	1.7
	Price			-0.4	1.6	1.2	3.2	-2.9	-2.1	-2.4	1.6	4.0	4.5	5.8

1. Index II: excluding precious metals, previous stones, works of art and antiques.
Source: Banque nationale suisse, Bulletin mensuel.

32

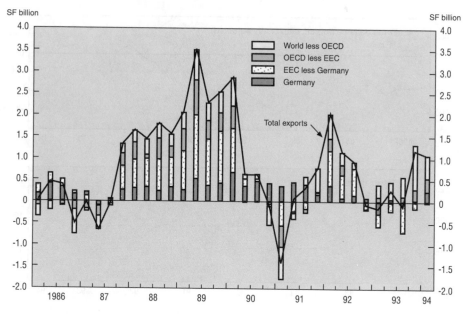

Diagram 11. **REGIONAL DISAGGREGATION OF CHANGES IN EXPORTS**

Change over the same quarter of previous year

Source: OECD, *Monthly Statistics of Foreign Trade.*

demand, thereby also serving as a valuable early indicator of domestic trends. Total merchandise import volumes fell by an annual average rate of 1.2 per cent in 1993 (less than in 1992), reflecting declining purchases of investment goods and production inputs, while consumer goods imports recovered from the second quarter of 1993 onward. The turnaround of total domestic demand during the second half of 1993 and in the first quarter of 1994 induced a pick-up of import volumes for investment goods, raw materials and semi-finished goods towards the end of 1993 and in the first quarter of 1994. But for 1993 as a whole, the (fob-cif) trade account, which is usually in deficit, turned into a surplus of SF 2.9 billion, the first surplus since 1976. Seasonally-adjusted data suggest that the trade surplus declined in the second half of 1993 in line with developments observed during previous cyclical recoveries. However, due to the continuing improvement

Diagram 12. **FOREIGN TRADE INDICATORS**

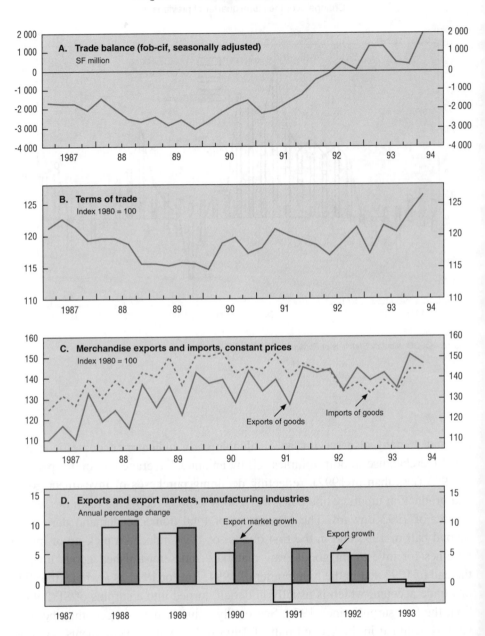

A. **Trade balance (fob-cif, seasonally adjusted)**
SF million

B. **Terms of trade**
Index 1980 = 100

C. **Merchandise exports and imports, constant prices**
Index 1980 = 100

Exports of goods

Imports of goods

D. **Exports and export markets, manufacturing industries**
Annual percentage change

Export market growth

Export growth

Source: OECD.

34

in the terms of trade, the trade surplus rose again in the first quarter of 1994 (Diagram 12).

The surplus in the services account continued to grow, owing to rising banking commissions, higher net revenues from tourism, lower net labour income paid abroad and higher net investment income. Altogether the current external surplus widened further, by SF 6½ billion to SF 27.6 billion (8.0 per cent of GDP) in 1993 (Table 6). It continued to increase in the first quarter of 1994 (to SF 9.4 billion, not s.a.).

Table 6. **Balance of payments**

$ billion

	1991	1992	1993	1992		1993	
				I	II	I	II
Seasonally adjusted[1]							
Exports (fob)	63.4	67.8	65.5	32.6	35.2	32.5	33.0
Imports (fob)	65.5	65.1	60.4	31.8	33.3	29.6	30.8
Trade balance	−2.1	2.7	5.0	0.8	1.9	2.8	2.2
Services	15.3	15.3	16.3	7.1	8.2	8.1	8.2
Private transfers, net	−2.3	−2.4	−2.2	−1.2	−1.2	−1.0	−1.2
Official transfers, net	−0.3	−0.6	−0.6	−0.3	−0.3	−0.2	−0.3
Current balance	10.6	15.0	18.6	6.5	8.6	9.7	9.0
Not seasonally adjusted							
Current balance	10.6	15.1	18.6	7.3	7.7	10.5	8.2
Non-monetary capital	−14.7	−6.0					
Balance on non-monetary	−4.1	9.1					
Short-term monetary capital	5.1	−4.6					
Balance on official settlements	1.0	4.4					
Memorandum items (SF billion)							
Tourism	2.8	2.9	3.5				
Capital movements	−13.8	−14.9					
Non-monetary capital	−21.0	−8.4					
Bank capital	7.2	−6.5					
Balance on official settlements	1.4	6.2					
Trade balance[2]	−8.0	−1.0	2.9				
Current balance	15.1	21.2	27.6				

1. Seasonal adjustment by the OECD. 1992 and 1993 figures are still preliminary.
2. Exports (fob) minus imports (cif).
Source: Banque nationale suisse, *Bulletin mensuel;* OECD.

The outlook to 1995

Current indicators

Most current and forward-looking indicators suggest that the Swiss economy turned around during the second half of 1993 and is now on an upward trend. The KOF (Zürich) business climate indicator began to pick up as early as in July 1993 – albeit from a very low level – and has improved since then. It approached the range generally considered "normal" by entrepreneurs at the beginning of 1994, after having stayed in the zone labelled "unfavourable" for nearly three years. Also starting from an extremely depressed level, the balance of incoming orders improved fairly steadily during 1993 and became positive from January 1994 on. As a consequence, the stock of orders – although still assessed as unsatisfactory – also signalled some amelioration. Business expectations for the three months ahead improved markedly and are now for an expansion of production. Industrial capacity utilisation appears to be on an upward trend. Clear signs of improving consumer confidence emerged in late 1993 and in the first half of 1994 (Diagram 13), a particularly important development in view of the weakness of private consumption expenditure and the dominant weight of this component in total demand. The consumer survey indicates that households' assessment of the overall economic situation became less pessimistic and that consumers adopted a more sanguine view of their own financial status.

Policy assumptions

The projections discussed below have been worked out on the technical assumption of nominal exchange rates remaining unchanged at their levels of 10 May 1994. Consequent upon its upward drift during most of 1993 and in the first four months of 1994, this implies that the Swiss franc would appreciate on average by 4¾ per cent in nominal effective terms in 1994. With the growth of the seasonally-adjusted monetary base below the Swiss National Bank's medium-term target, it is assumed that over the projection period short-term interest rates may decline somewhat further. With other European money market interest rates – in particular Deutschemark rates – also projected to decline, and with the success achieved on the inflation front, further monetary ease is likely to be compatible with the technical assumption of a stable external value of the Swiss franc. Consequent upon the fall in bond prices in world capital markets since

36

Diagram 13. **INDICATORS OF ACTIVITY**

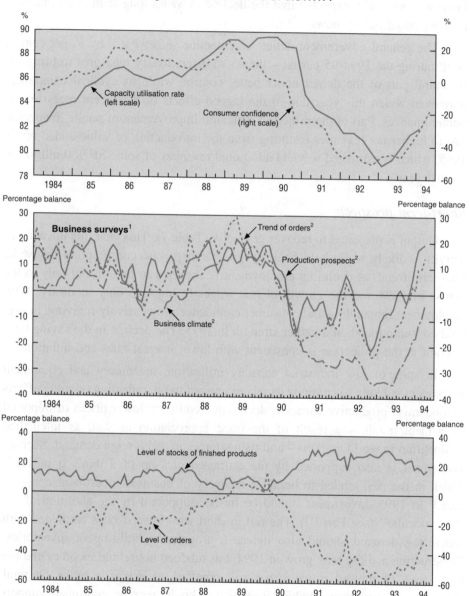

1. Balance of positive and negative orders.
2. 3-month moving average.
Source: KOF/ETH, *Konjunktur,* and OECD, *Main Economic Indicators.*

February 1994, it is expected that the decline in Swiss long-term bond rates has nearly petered out by now.

The general government deficit may decline somewhat – by ¾ per cent of GDP during the 1994-95 period – thanks to discretionary measures to bring the structural part of the deficit under better control, while its cyclical component may even widen this year due to the lagged effects of the recent recession on public finances. Part of the projected structural improvement of public finances is due to higher tax revenues resulting from the introduction of value-added tax in 1995, which is estimated to yield additional revenues of some SF 900 million in its first year.

Short-term prospects

Output is projected to recover gradually (Table 7). This year, the upswing of activity is likely to be held back by growth in private consumption below its long-term trend, as declining employment is expected to bottom out only in the course of 1994 and the growth of real wages to improve only modestly. With employment rebounding and consumer confidence progressively reviving, house-hold consumption should gather strength in 1995. The decline in the saving ratio implicit in the projection is consistent with lower interest rates and inflation.

In spite of low industrial capacity utilisation, machinery and equipment investment is likely to continue its recent upward trend, reflecting ongoing efforts to modernise productive capacity, declining credit cost, lower prices of imported investment goods – a result of the franc appreciation as well as intensified competition in world markets – and rising domestic and foreign demand. Such an assessment is also supported by the estimated pick-up of Tobin's q in 1993, which in the past tended to herald a recovery of business investment one year later.[14] In 1995, investment should be further supported by the abolition of the "taxe occulte" (see Part III). The fall in short-term interest rates combined with recovering demand should also induce a progressive build-up of inventories. Construction activity may grow in 1994, but subdued household incomes and the high stock of unused office space will continue to act as a brake on total construction investment. Public investment should receive continued support from the "investment bonus programme".

Exports are likely to strengthen, reflecting vigorous growth of export mar-kets. The detrimental effect of exchange rate appreciation on price competitive-

Table 7. **Short-term projections**

	Current prices SF billion 1991	Share of GDP	Percentage changes			
			1992	1993	1994[1]	1995[1]
Demand and output (volume)[2]						
Private consumption	190.5	57.5	−0.2	−0.8	1.0	1.8
Public consumption	46.6	14.1	0.5	−0.4	1.0	1.3
Gross fixed capital formation	84.8	25.6	−5.0	−4.3	2.4	4.7
Construction	55.9	16.9	−2.3	−4.2	1.0	2.5
Machinery and equipment	28.9	8.7	−9.6	−4.3	5.0	8.5
Final domestic demand	321.9	97.2	−1.4	−1.7	1.4	2.5
Change in stocks[3, 4]	4.5	1.4	−1.7	0.3	0.5	0.7
Total domestic demand	326.5	98.6	−3.0	−1.4	1.9	3.1
Exports of goods and services	116.7	35.3	3.4	0.8	3.5	5.0
Imports of goods and services	112.1	33.9	−3.8	−1.2	4.2	6.2
Change in foreign balance[3]	4.6	1.4	3.2	0.9	−0.4	−0.7
Gross domestic product	333.1	100.0	−0.1	−0.5	1.5	2.5
Industrial production			−0.7	−1.0	1.8	3.1
Prices						
GDP deflator			2.5	2.5	1.8	2.8
Private consumption deflator			4.1	2.9	1.0	2.5
Unemployment rate			2.5	4.5	4.5	3.8
Current balance ($ billion)			15.0	18.6	18.3	18.0
Per cent of GDP			6.2	8.0	7.3	6.8

1. OECD forecast.
2. At 1980 prices.
3. As a percentage of previous year's GDP.
4. Including statistical adjustments.
Source: Swiss national accounts; OECD.

ness should be partly offset by favourable unit labour cost developments and price concessions by Swiss producers. As import demand picks up on the back of strengthening domestic demand, the real foreign balance will deteriorate, making a small negative growth contribution to growth this year and next. With the terms of trade improving further and net investment income remaining buoyant, the current external surplus is likely to decline only slowly, to around 7 per cent of GDP in 1994 and 1995.

The recorded average annual rate of unemployment may stabilise in 1994 as the projected contraction of employment is expected to be offset by a reduction in the labour supply, in particular a fall in the number of seasonal and frontier workers. The labour market should show clearer signs of improvement in 1995, when higher capacity utilisation calls for growing labour input. Given the recent exchange rate appreciation and the existing slack in the economy, consumer price inflation is set to slow down again in 1994, to an average rate of 1 per cent. Underlying inflation will remain very low in 1995, but the replacement of the present retail sales tax on goods by a general value-added tax at the beginning of 1995 could raise recorded CPI inflation temporarily to 2½ per cent in 1995.

Risks and uncertainties

Risks to the projections appear to be evenly balanced. Private consumption might be underestimated as consumer confidence could improve faster and the household propensity to save decline by more than implied in the projection. On the other hand, business investment decisions remain subject to uncertainty related to the role Switzerland will play in the process of European integration. Construction activity might be impaired by high real interest rates if the recent sharp increase in long-term interest turned out to be permanent.

II. Economic policy

The role of macroeconomic policies

Swiss macroeconomic policies are guided by a commitment to a stable policy environment, which has been recognised as a precondition for steady economic growth and low inflation. To bring this about, fiscal policy aims at providing essential public services within a balanced budget over the medium term. Swiss authorities do not consider fiscal policy as a suitable instrument of cyclical stabilisation. The efficacy of active fiscal policy is in any case constrained by the fact that the Swiss public sector is relatively small and that the federal government accounts for only one-third of it. In addition, taxation is subject to direct democratic control and the length of time involved in collecting direct taxes is considerable.

Monetary policy seeks to ensure steady growth of the money supply through the setting of a stable objective for base money growth. A salient feature of the Swiss approach to monetary targeting is the directness of the control of the monetary base, exercised through the use of currency swaps, whereby the National Bank buys or sells foreign exchange for a predetermined period of time from commercial banks. However, recent legislative and technological changes in the financial sector have raised doubts about the stability of the link between the monetary base and broad money supply. Although targeting the growth of the monetary base is the centre-piece of monetary policy, the National Bank has stressed on a number of occasions the need for some flexibility in the application of the strategy, in particular deviations from base money targets would be tolerated to counteract excessive exchange rate changes.

Gradual relaxation of monetary conditions

Monetary targets and actual developments

After falling short of its annual targets by substantial margins from 1988 to 1990, the Swiss National Bank (SNB) suspended its yearly targeting practice and announced as its new intermediate objective an expansion of the seasonally-adjusted monetary base[15] (SAMB) of 1 per cent *per annum* over the medium term, defined as a period of three to five years. Such modest expansion of the SAMB is in accordance with the current trend growth of notes in circulation, which now account for 91 per cent of the monetary base: the growth rate of notes slowed down from $2\frac{1}{2}$ per cent *per annum* during most of the 1980s to 1 per cent thereafter (Diagram 14), in part presumably as a result of the continuing technical progress in payments transactions. The SNB considers the targeted low expansion of base money compatible with real economic growth along the path of potential output, which the SNB puts at 2 per cent, and a consumer price inflation objective of 0 to 1 per cent. The fourth quarter of 1989 was set as base period of the targeting exercise[16] although it was not clear to what degree a new equilibrium between the demand for base money and its key determinants – real growth, prices and interest rates – had been re-established by late 1989. The demand for bank notes, however, which at that time already amounted to about 90 per cent of base money, had barely been affected by the institutional changes of 1988.

In the event, instead of growing, the SAMB declined by an annual average of 0.7 per cent from 1990 to 1992 – the first three years of the exercise – reflecting broad stagnation of notes in circulation, tighter base money supply and further contraction of banks' demand for Central Bank money. The latter was due to the ongoing adjustment of the banks' liquidity management to the implementation of the Swiss Interbank Clearing system (SIC) and the introduction of new prudential liquidity regulations[17] in 1988, which reduced drastically the banks' need for base money. According to SNB estimates, this further downward adjustment in the demand for base money amounted to about 1 per cent in the 1990-92 period. The decline in the demand for base money in 1990 to 1992 appears all the more remarkable as *nominal* incomes continued to grow strongly and short-term interest rates were on a slight downward trend during 1990 and 1991; apart from a temporary surge during the spring and the summer, interest rates kept on falling also during 1992. But interest rates on savings deposits, to

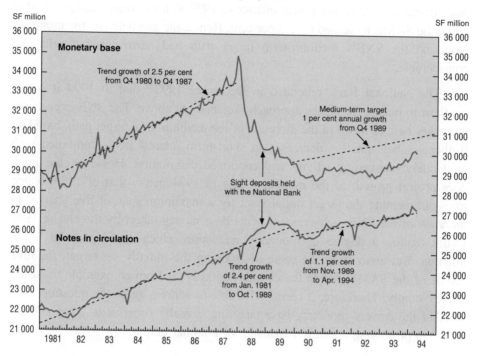

Diagram 14. **THE ADJUSTED MONETARY BASE**
Seasonally adjusted

SF million

Monetary base

Trend growth of 2.5 per cent
from Q4 1980 to Q4 1987

Medium-term target
1 per cent annual growth
from Q4 1989

Sight deposits held
with the National Bank

Notes in circulation

Trend growth
of 2.4 per cent
from Jan. 1981
to Oct. 1989

Trend growth
of 1.1 per cent
from Nov. 1989
to Apr. 1994

Source: Banque nationale suisse, *Bulletin mensuel.*

which Swiss demand for bank notes reacts most strongly, still rose considerably in 1990 and began falling only in early 1993.

For 1993, the National Bank projected the growth of the monetary base to distinctly exceed the medium-term target rate. This was based on expectations of unchanged economic activity, further progress on the inflation front and a continuation of the decrease in interest rates. Although interest rates and inflation developed broadly in line with the SNB's projections, output contracted further, so that the demand for notes grew by an average annual rate of only 1.5 per cent while the banks' sight deposits edged up by 4 per cent, the first positive rate of growth since 1987. But as a consequence of the reduced weight of the latter component, the average annual increase in the monetary base only amounted to

43

1.7 per cent in 1993. In the course of 1993, however, the growth of monetary base accelerated: from the fourth quarter of 1992 to the corresponding period in 1993, the SAMB increased by 2.8 per cent. Hence, the gap between the monetary base and the SNB's medium-term target path had narrowed, but remained considerable.

The National Bank reiterated in December 1993[18] that in 1994 it would continue to pursue the policy approach sketched out above. The SNB expects the monetary base to move in the direction of the medium-term target path, based on further – albeit small – decreases in short-term interest rates, combined with moderately recovering activity and continued disinflation. However, the Bank does project growth of the monetary base in 1994 below that of 1993, which rules out meeting the target initially set for a maximum span of five years.[19] In the view of the SNB, achievement of its base money target by the end of 1994 would require a degree of monetary relaxation which could provoke future inflation. But apart from the issue of attaining the initially set target, the time profile of the SAMB during the chosen period is far from an example of steady money supply. Therefore, it seems advisable to address again the question as to whether the current monetary-base targeting is really superior to other alternatives[20] in promoting a steady expansion of nominal output.

Broader monetary aggregates

Broader monetary aggregates displayed a rather divergent picture of monetary conditions in 1993 after having shown unequivocal signs of monetary tightness in 1992: following its stagnation in 1992, M1 picked up by almost 10 per cent in 1993, boosted by soaring demand for sight deposits, which is not unusual for the end of a recession period, when inflation and money market interest rates decline. Indications of a normalisation of demand for M1 were registered in the spring of 1994. Following the drop of short-term interest rates, sight deposit accounts were nourished from funds flowing out of time deposits; the latter contracted sharply and induced M2 to decrease (Table 8). Shifts out of longer-term instruments (bank bonds, for example) and out of time deposits as well as an apparent increase in the households' propensity to save are mirrored in the accelerated expansion of savings deposits from 5½ per cent in 1992 to 20 per cent in 1993; this nearly doubled the growth rate of the broad aggregate M3 to

Table 8. **Monetary aggregates and income velocity of money**

| | 1988 | 1989 | 1990 | 1991 | 1992 | 1993 | 1993 | | | | 1994 |
							Q1	Q2	Q3	Q4	Q1
						Percentage change from previous year					
Notes in circulation	4.2	2.4	-2.1	2.2	0.1	1.5	1.3	1.1	1.5	2.3	1.6
Sight deposits held with SNB	-34.5	-38.5	-13.5	-6.2	-9.9	3.9	2.2	1.8	7.3	4.6	6.4
Adjusted monetary base (AMB)[1]	-5.6	-5.0	-3.4	1.3	-0.9	1.7	1.4	1.1	2.0	2.5	2.0
Sight deposits	18.6	-8.7	-5.3	0.5	0.3	13.3	9.4	13.8	16.5	13.6	13.5
M1	14.2	-5.5	-4.2	1.2	0.1	9.5	6.7	9.6	11.6	9.9	9.7
Time deposits	0.7	50.9	26.0	4.4	0.9	-17.1	-9.4	-18.7	-21.2	-18.7	-12.7
M2	7.6	20.1	13.0	3.2	0.5	-7.6	-3.6	-8.8	-10.0	-8.0	-3.8
Savings deposits	11.6	-5.1	-8.5	3.1	5.6	20.2	13.9	19.7	23.8	23.3	19.0
M3	9.8	6.2	2.4	3.2	2.8	5.0	4.3	4.0	5.1	6.5	7.6
Domestic credit expansion	11.3	14.5	11.8	6.7	4.4	1.3	1.3	1.0	1.6	1.3	1.5
Nominal GDP	5.4	8.2	8.1	5.4	2.5	2.0	1.1	1.7	2.4	2.5	4.2
						Percentage change in income velocity					
GDP/AMB[1]	11.9	13.8	12.0	4.1	3.4	0.2	-0.3	0.6	0.5	0.0	2.2
GDP/M1	-7.7	14.4	12.9	4.2	2.6	-6.9	-5.3	-7.2	-8.2	-6.7	-5.0
GDP/M2	-2.1	-9.9	-4.3	2.1	2.0	10.4	4.9	11.5	13.8	11.5	8.3
GDP/M3	-4.0	1.9	5.6	2.2	-0.2	-2.9	-3.1	-2.2	-2.5	-3.7	-3.1

1. Change of definition in 1989.
Source: Banque nationale suisse, *Bulletin mensuel*; OECD.

45

5.0 per cent in 1993, well ahead of the expansion of nominal GDP. M3 growth even accelerated in the first four months of 1994.

However, signals from broader aggregates need to be interpreted with caution. In particular, M1, which the SNB emphasises as a particularly meaningful additional indicator of monetary policy,[21] may have given a misleading picture of the degree of relaxation due to the well-known problem of non-inclusion of the so-called salary accounts,[22] which are widely used for transaction purposes and should thus be counted in M1. In addition, M1 – as well as M2 and M3 – was temporarily distorted by the erroneous inclusion of liabilities ensuing from securities lending in the commercial banks' reports on demand and time deposits.[23] The revised growth rates of monetary aggregates are up to more than 3 percentage points below the initial figures.

Short-term interest and exchange rates

With uncertainty about the indicative quality of customary monetary aggregates, interest and exchange rates remain key variables in the evaluation of recent monetary conditions in Switzerland. The exchange rate plays a particularly prominent role since the high degree of openness of the Swiss economy makes domestic prices susceptible to changes in the exchange rate and provides thereby a powerful instrument for stabilisation policies. However, recent movements of interest and exchange rates provide a rather mixed picture of monetary conditions since they reflect not only the monetary policy stance but also a variety of other factors.

In view of the lags between the application of monetary policy instruments and their effects on the economy, the National Bank allowed short-term interest rates to decrease from early 1990 and during the following 26 months, with only short-lived interruptions (Diagram 15). This process came to an end when the negative short-term Swiss franc-Deutschemark interest rate differential had widened to an extent that triggered an acceleration of the downward drift of the Swiss franc effective exchange rate. In the course of the first half of 1992, the franc exchange rate fell back to its low level of the second half of 1989, implying an effective depreciation by some 5 per cent during the first five months of 1992. Concerned about higher import price inflation, the National Bank tightened its policy stance again, in order to prop up the franc's external value. The support for the exchange rate from rebounding interest rates was accentuated by strong

Diagram 15. **INTEREST AND EXCHANGE RATES**

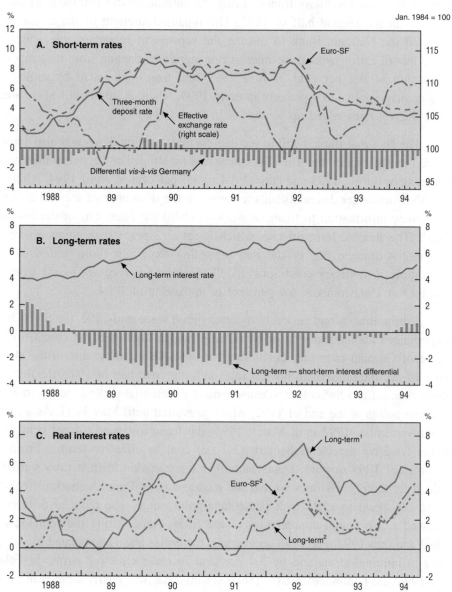

1. Nominal rate less the change in the wholesale price index from the previous year.
2. Nominal rate less the change in the consumer price index from the previous year.
Source: OECD, *Main Economic Indicators,* and estimates.

foreign demand for Swiss francs during the turbulences in European exchange markets in the second half of 1992. The regained strength of the Swiss franc allowed the National Bank to resume the process of monetary relaxation: the three-month Euro-Swiss franc interest rate started to decline from its temporary maximum of 9.2 per cent in June 1992 and has since fallen by more than 5 percentage points to 4 per cent in early 1994, where it stood until May. Short-term interest rates edged up somewhat in June 1994.

The National Bank's will to see interest rates coming down was also demonstrated by the cuts in the official discount rate by altogether $2\frac{1}{2}$ percentage points in six steps during 1993 and early 1994 to $3\frac{1}{2}$ per cent in April 1994. Although the SNB no longer discounts bills, changes in the discount rate are still believed to convey information to financial markets about the intentions of the National Bank. The flexible lombard rate, which is set at 2 percentage points above the call-money interest rate of the two preceding days, also bore witness to the relaxation of monetary conditions. It fell by some 5 percentage points from the summer of 1992 to about $6\frac{1}{4}$ per cent in the spring of 1994.

During this second period of monetary ease since mid-1992, the Swiss franc experienced another episode of weakening, which highlights the crucial importance of German monetary conditions for the SNB's policy: due to the slower pace of decline of German interest rates in the second half of 1992, the negative three-month Euro-Swiss franc-Deutschemark differential widened to $2\frac{3}{4}$ to 3 percentage points at the end of 1992, which prevailed until May 1993. As a result, from September 1992 until March 1993, the franc lost nearly 4 per cent of its value *vis-à-vis* the Deutschemark (3.7 per cent in effective terms). From the summer of 1993 onward, Deutschemark money market interest rates started to fall faster than Swiss rates so that the negative franc-Deutschemark differential narrowed again to a $1\frac{1}{2}$ to 2 percentage-point range. The reduced differential allowed a substantial appreciation of the Swiss franc during the remainder of 1993 and into 1994. For 1993 on average, the Swiss franc appreciated by 4.1 per cent in nominal terms and by 3.4 per cent in real[24] effective terms. In February 1994, the nominal effective franc exchange rate was nearly 8 per cent higher than twelve months ago; in real terms it even exceeded its previous peak of late 1987. The Swiss franc remained very strong in the second quarter of 1994. Hence, seen from this angle and in spite of the substantial drop of short-term interest rates since the summer of 1992, the SNB's monetary policy stance still appears relatively restrictive. The remaining degree of monetary tightness has until recently also been reflected in the slope of the "yield curve" (the term structure of interest rates): after having remained distinctly negative for as long as 45 consecutive months, it turned flat in late 1992 and remained so for most of 1993. Only from late 1993 onward did the yield curve exhibit a slightly positive slope. The increased steepness of the yield curve from February to June 1994 is a reflection of developments in international capital markets rather than induced by Swiss monetary policy.

Capital market interest rates

Starting from a peak of roughly 7 per cent in mid-1992, the highest level since 1974, the Confederation bond rate decreased fairly rapidly to slightly above 4 per cent in late 1993 and in early 1994. A reverse movement of the Swiss bond rate occurred between February and June 1994 when international capital markets responded to steps of monetary tightening in the United States so that the Confederation bond rate moved up again to 5¼ per cent in June 1994. The fall in mortgage interest rates, which had started in the second half of 1992, persisted during 1993 and into 1994 as banks continued to pass on to their clients the reduced cost of bank refinancing. Interest rates on new mortgages decreased particularly rapidly, by some 2¼ per cent from their peak level in the autumn of 1992 to 5½ per cent in the first half of 1994. This may not only reflect the banking sectors' collective efforts to revive depressed credit demand, but may also bear witness to the intensified competition among banks after the dismantling of cartel arrangements in the banking sector.[25]

Movements in long-term interest rates may be assessed in the light of latest econometric estimates[26] of the OECD Secretariat: the results obtained suggest that the drop in the Confederation bond rate until the end of 1993 was brought about not only by easier monetary conditions in Switzerland as indicated by lower Swiss franc short-term interest rates, but also by the decline in the German bond rate, the growing current external surplus (relative to GDP) and the fall in Swiss consumer price inflation to below the German inflation rate (Diagram 16). The equation also suggests that Swiss long-term interest rates tend to decline when growth is below that in Germany, but – although statistically highly significant – the impact is comparatively small.

Diagram 16. **THE DETERMINANTS OF THE SWISS LONG-TERM INTEREST RATE**

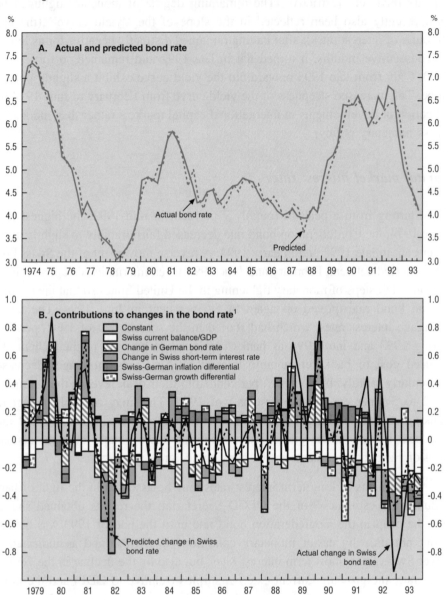

1. The decomposition of the change in the bond rate refers to the equation presented in footnote 26.
Source: OECD.

The recently observed uncoupling of Swiss long-term interest rates from those abroad seems to suggest that earlier concerns about the end of Switzerland's status as an "island" of exceptionally low interest rates (*"îlot des taux d'intérêts"*) were not warranted. This debate[27] had been provoked by short- and long-term interest rates which were unusually high both in absolute terms as well as relative to other countries – especially Germany – in the late 1980s and in the early 1990s. Although work of the OECD Secretariat to estimate an explicit model of the long-term interest differential between Switzerland and abroad led to rather inconclusive results, it is possible to detect a statistically significant trend increase in the differential from the second quarter of 1990 onward. However, the equation for changes in the Confederation bond rate presented above allows a *partial* answer to the question as to the conditions under which Swiss interest rates tend to be lower than abroad, namely – *ceteris paribus* – a better inflation performance, which then allows lower short-term interest rates in Switzerland than elsewhere, a current external surplus, and slower economic growth than abroad.

Conventionally measured real long-term interest rates came down from their peak of 3¼ per cent in the summer of 1992 to below 1 per cent twelve months later. But with bond rates falling less rapidly than prices and even picking up again in the first half of 1994, real long-term interest rates turned round again and reached a level of nearly 5 per cent in June 1994. Although they remain among the lowest in the OECD (Table 9), their current level is substantially higher than in early 1983, when the previous cyclical upswing took place. Real short-term interest rates display a similar picture: from their high level of about 5 per cent in the middle of 1992, they declined to nearly 1 per cent in mid-1993, but picked up again to 3½ per cent in the summer of 1994. This is in clear contrast to the beginning of the preceding two economic upswings – early 1976 and late 1982 – when significantly negative short-term interest rates supported the recovery.

Moreover, when assessing the impact of monetary conditions on business investment decisions, consumer price inflation may be a misleading indicator for entrepreneurial inflation expectations. Expected producer prices may be more pertinent to the assessment of the business sector's real credit cost. If expected producer prices are approximated by the current rate of producer price inflation – which is zero or even negative – the real long-term interest rate still appears substantial relative to its own past values (see the bottom panel of Diagram 15

Table 9.   **Nominal and real interest rates in selected OECD countries.**

	1991	1992	1993	1992 Q1	1992 Q2	1992 Q3	1992 Q4	1993 Q1	1993 Q2	1993 Q3	1993 Q4	1994 Q1	1994 Q2
							Short-term rates [1]						
Nominal rates													
Switzerland	7.6	7.2	4.3	7.4	8.6	7.2	5.7	4.8	4.5	4.1	3.8	3.5	3.6
United States	5.9	3.8	3.3	4.2	4.0	3.4	3.6	3.3	3.3	3.3	3.4	3.7	4.7
Germany	9.2	9.5	7.3	9.6	9.8	9.7	9.0	8.3	7.7	6.8	6.4	5.9	5.3
Japan	7.2	4.3	2.9	5.1	4.6	3.9	3.7	3.4	3.2	3.0	2.2	2.1	2.2
United Kingdom	11.5	9.6	5.9	10.5	10.2	10.2	7.6	6.4	5.9	5.9	5.6	5.3	5.2
France	9.6	10.3	8.6	10.1	10.0	10.6	10.7	11.8	8.0	7.8	6.7	6.3	5.7
							Long-term rates [2]						
Switzerland	6.2	6.4	4.6	6.3	6.8	6.7	5.8	5.0	4.7	4.4	4.1	4.3	4.9
United States	7.9	7.0	5.9	7.3	7.4	6.6	6.7	6.3	6.0	5.6	5.6	6.1	7.1
Germany	8.6	7.9	6.3	8.1	8.1	8.0	7.3	6.7	6.6	6.2	5.8	6.1	6.7
Japan	6.4	5.3	4.3	5.5	5.7	5.0	4.9	4.4	4.8	4.2	3.6	4.2	8.3
United Kingdom	10.1	9.1	7.5	9.5	9.2	9.2	8.4	8.0	8.0	7.2	6.7	6.8	7.4
France	9.5	9.0	7.0	9.0	9.1	9.4	8.5	8.0	7.4	6.7	6.1	6.4	7.4
							Short-term						
Inflation-adjusted rates [3]													
Switzerland	1.8	3.2	1.0	2.6	4.2	3.6	2.3	1.2	1.0	0.7	1.2	1.8	2.9
United States	1.6	0.8	0.4	1.3	0.9	0.3	0.5	0.1	0.1	0.6	0.6	1.2	2.3
Germany	5.8	5.5	3.2	5.3	5.3	6.3	5.3	4.0	3.5	2.7	2.6	2.5	2.3
Japan	3.9	2.7	1.8	3.3	2.4	2.2	3.0	2.2	2.5	1.3	1.2	1.0	1.7
United Kingdom	5.6	5.9	4.4	6.4	6.1	6.5	4.5	4.5	4.7	4.3	4.0	2.9	2.6
France	6.4	8.0	6.5	7.3	7.3	8.4	8.9	9.7	6.0	5.6	4.6	4.6	4.0
							Long-term						
Switzerland	0.4	2.4	1.3	1.5	2.4	3.1	2.4	1.5	1.2	1.0	1.5	2.7	4.3
United States	3.6	4.0	2.9	4.4	4.3	3.5	3.7	3.1	2.8	2.9	2.9	3.6	4.7
Germany	5.1	3.9	2.2	3.8	3.6	4.5	3.6	2.4	2.4	2.0	2.1	2.8	3.7
Japan	3.1	3.7	3.1	3.7	3.5	3.3	4.1	3.2	4.1	2.5	2.6	3.1	3.6
United Kingdom	4.3	5.3	5.9	5.4	5.0	5.6	5.3	6.2	6.7	5.6	5.1	4.4	5.8
France	6.3	6.6	4.9	6.2	6.3	7.2	6.6	5.9	5.4	4.5	4.0	4.7	5.7

1.   Domestic rates, mostly for 3 months.
2.   Government bond rates, except in Germany and France, where rates are respectively for public sector bonds and for public sector and semi-public sector bonds.
3.   Nominal rates less the annual change in consumer prices.
Source: OECD, *Monthly Financial Statistics* and *Main Economic Indicators.*

52

above). It is markedly higher than interest rates deflated by the consumer price index.

Is there scope for further monetary easing?

In spite of the high degree of price stability now achieved, other problems remain, most importantly high unemployment. Although it is widely recognised that artificially easy monetary conditions would only offer a temporary boost to activity and would incur unacceptably high welfare costs in the medium term, the question remains as to what is the appropriate stance of monetary policy. This is all the more so as in Switzerland, as in other OECD countries, legal and techno-logical change in financial markets has raised doubts about the stability of formerly reliable indicators of monetary conditions. In particular, the recent break in the demand for base money and still insufficient experience as to its present quantitative link with key macroeconomic variables makes too heavy reliance on this indicator a risky option. Of course, the potential for the banks' sight deposits held with the SNB to bring the base money off its target trajectory has been reduced substantially by its falling share in the monetary base from over 25 per cent in 1987 – just before the structural break – down to about 9 per cent in 1992/93. But rather than being a virtue, the reduced weight of bank liquidity in the National Bank's intermediate target aggregate embodies the risk of weaken-ing the link between the SNB's operations and the "real side" of the economy. On the other hand, customary broader monetary aggregates all suffer from seri-ous flaws which make them rather auxiliary instruments of monetary analysis. Therefore, at the current juncture it seems useful to look – as in other OECD countries – at a broad spectrum of monetary indicators. In doing so, the follow-ing summary picture emerges:

- in the summer of 1994, the adjusted monetary base is well below the National Bank's medium-term target path and, although the gap was narrowing during the first half of the year, it is unlikely to be closed by the end of 1994;
- the demand for notes in circulation has remained subdued, in spite of the decline in interest rates. However, it grew at a rate of 4.8 per cent (s.a.a.r) in the first quarter of 1994;
- inflationary pressures are low now and are likely to remain so;
- real short- and long-term interest rates are still relatively high;

Diagram 17. **THE OUTPUT GAP**

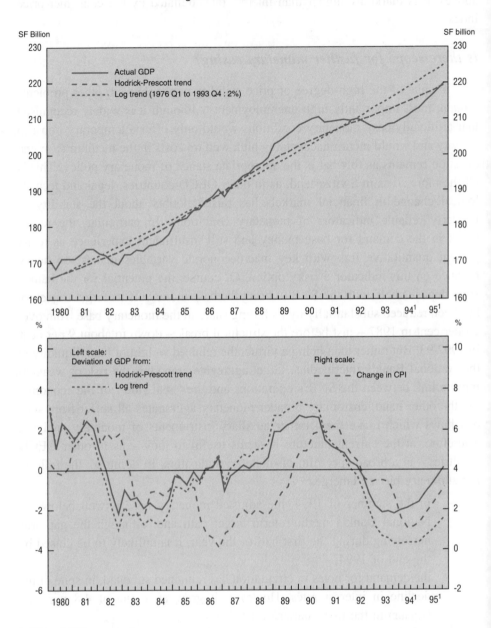

1. 1994 and 1995 are projections.
Source: OECD.

- the yield curve was relatively flat until early 1994. With long-term interest rates increasing since February 1994, the yield curve has returned to a normal positive slope, but this reflects developments in world capital markets rather than a change in the Swiss policy setting;
- the Swiss franc exchange rate is unusually high – by past standards and when adjusted for relative consumer price or unit labour cost differentials;
- alternative approaches indicate that the absolute difference between actual output and its estimated potential, the "output gap", is still substantial (Diagram 17). The gap was of the order of 4 per cent of potential output in late 1993 if a long term linear trend is used for comparison. A flexible trend may be applied to reflect the argument that part of the productive potential disintegrates during periods of slack. Even on this basis, the output gap would still amount to somewhat over 2 per cent in the fourth quarter of 1993.

The combination of all these indicators suggests that there would still be some scope for monetary easing. The OECD Secretariat projections presented above assume that this room will be used by monetary authorities. On this basis, the gap between actual output and its linear trend will narrow but not close during the projection period, while real GDP will reach potential output as represented by the flexible trend by the end of 1995. The projected rise in inflation in 1995 does not result from the closing output gap but is due to a temporary effect of the introduction of VAT.

Widening government deficits

Overview

Government finances deteriorated further in 1993: instead of keeping the deficit at the projected SF 11 billion, the consolidated accounts of Confederation, cantons and communes closed with a deficit of SF 16.2 billion (Table 10). Including the social security system, the general government deficit rose by 1 percentage point to 4.5 per cent of GDP in 1993. As in previous years, most of the worsening of public finances occurred at the Confederation level. But the cantons also widened their deficit by another SF 0.5 billion instead of the

Table 10. Government accounts

SF million and percentage changes

	1990	Outturns			Budgets[1]	
	SF million	1991	1992	1993	1993	1994
Confederation						
Expenditure	31 616	12.3	6.5	7.4	7.1	7.2
Revenue	30 837	2.0	4.2	−4.2	2.4	−1.8
Balance	−779	−4 044	−5 039	−9 199	−4 688	−8 166
Cantons						
Expenditure	41 413	11.0	6.1	–	6.2	6.2
Revenue	39 561	6.6	5.7	–	5.6	4.4
Balance	−1 852	−3 781	−4 163	−4 795	−4 200	−5 300
Communes						
Expenditure	30 245	9.9	7.1	–	7.9	4.3
Revenue	29 423	5.7	7.1	–	4.7	4.3
Balance	−822	−2 151	−2 300	−2 250	−2 400	−2 500
General government[2]						
Expenditure	86 614	11.2	6.6	–	7.1	5.6
Revenue	83 161	3.8	5.6	–	4.0	1.4
Balance	−3 453	−9 976	−11 502	−16 244	−11 288	−15 966
As a percentage of GDP	−1.1	−3.0	−3.4	−4.7	–	–
Social security						
Expenditure	26 358	11.3	15.3	–	–	–
Revenue	29 686	8.6	4.9	–	–	–
Balance	+3 328	+2 917	+27	+659	–	–
Consolidated account of general government and social security						
Expenditure	105 077	11.3	8.7	–	–	–
Revenue	104 952	4.7	5.2	–	–	–
Balance	−125	−7 059	−11 475	−17 040	–	–
As a percentage of GDP	−0.0	−2.1	−3.4	−4.5	–	–

1. Initial budget on initial budget.
2. Excluding social security.
Source: Administration fédérale des finances.

envisaged stabilisation, and latest estimates of a deficit of SF 2¼ billion in 1993 do not show any noteworthy improvement in the communes' finances either. The social security system[28] posted a surplus but this was only due to a transfer of SF 4.1 billion from Confederation and cantons to the unemployment insurance system.

Consequent upon the growing deficits, the Confederation's gross financial debt rose from 16¼ per cent of GDP in 1992 to about 20 per cent in 1993 (Diagram 18). Gross debt of the general government increased by a remarkable 6 percentage points to an estimated 43½ per cent of GDP at the end of 1993. Recent budget projections imply another jump to close to 47 per cent at the end of 1994. Although the gross debt/GDP ratio still remains low by international comparison[29] and is – for example – safely below the 60 per cent guideline laid out in the "Maastricht Treaty" for the European Monetary Union, its fast increase may give grounds for concern. Derived from a simple budget identity, a necessary condition for rapidly rising ("explosive") debt is a (real) growth rate of output below the (real) effective interest rate on public debt. In such a situation, interest payments add more to public debt than growth adds to GDP so that the debt-GDP ratio will rise unless there is a sufficiently high primary surplus, which was neither the case for general nor for federal government budget in the past three years. In 1992 and 1993, the nominal effective rate of interest on federal debt (4.6 and 3.7 per cent, respectively) was not only markedly above the

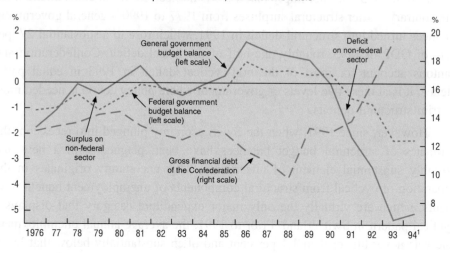

Diagram 18. **BUDGET BALANCES AND DEBT**

As per cent of GDP, transactions basis

1. Projection.
Source: Office fédéral des questions conjoncturelles.

57

growth rate of nominal GDP, but federal finances also recorded primary deficits in each year.[30]

Although the recent deterioration of government finances is substantial and must not be taken lightly, it should not be dramatised either. First, the weakening of federal tax revenues in an odd year of the biennial collection cycle of the federal direct tax[31] is a regular feature of Swiss public finances. Second, 1993 was the third and – in terms of foregone output – worst year of recession which – naturally – damped indirect tax revenues and raised expenditures for unemployment benefits.

Cyclically-adjusted budget balances

Decomposition of actual deficits into structural and cyclical parts[32] suggests that the structural deficit of the Confederation increased by about $1/4$ percentage point of GDP in 1993 while the fiscal policy stance of cantons and communes may be characterised as broadly neutral. In other words, almost all of the deterioration of actual government budget balances in 1993 is attributable to the cyclical downturn of the economy, so that it should be corrected with the economic recovery.

But the fact that no noteworthy structural deterioration of public finances occurred in 1993 does not imply that there is no need for fiscal consolidation. On the contrary – after structural surpluses from 1977 to 1990 – general government finances turned into structural deficit in 1991, which rose to a substantial $2^1/2$ per cent of GDP in 1993, roughly one-half of the actual deficit. Confederation and cantons account for most of the non-cyclical deficit in 1993 in equal parts. Hence, it is at these two levels of government where policy action is needed most to trim structural deficits.

However, since 1991, when the Swiss economy plunged into recession, the estimates of structural budget balances have been plagued with a new and possibly substantial element of uncertainty. This uncertainty originates in the separation of cyclical from structural components of unemployment benefit payments, which are virtually the only major expenditure category that displays a cyclical pattern in Switzerland. Prior to 1991, the average annual unemployment rate was never higher than 1.1 per cent and often substantially below that level. Estimates of the "non-accelerating-wage rate of unemployment" (NAWRU), based on expectations-augmented Phillips curves arrived at proxies for structural unemployment of about 0.8 per cent, which were used for calculations of structural budget balances until 1990. But the steep increase in unemployment since then despite a relatively mild slowdown in activity led to the widespread view that a substantial part of the rise in unemployment may be of a structural nature, a hypothesis which is supported by other indicators.[33] Because of an insufficient number of statistical observations, the quantification of the structural change is subject to a substantial error margin. The estimates used here assume that the non-cyclical rate of unemployment rose from 1½ per cent in 1992 to 2 per cent in 1993 and may stabilise at 2½ per cent thereafter. To the extent that the "true" non-cyclical rate of unemployment is higher, the structural part of the government budget deficit is underestimated, and budget consolidation would require even greater effort. The implied magnitudes can be gauged from 1993 data which suggest that unemployment benefits of SF 1.3 billion (0.4 per cent of GDP) have to be paid for each percentage point of the labour force which is unemployed.

The Confederation's finances in 1993

The budget deficit of the Confederation was projected to widen only a little in 1993, from an *actual* SF 2 863 million in 1992 to SF 3 087 million (0.9 per cent of GDP). This was based on the assumptions – established in mid-1992 – of 1.5 per cent real output growth and 3.5 per cent inflation. Although both output growth and inflation turned out to be significantly below what was expected, the realised growth of expenditures of 7.4 per cent met the budget projections with striking accuracy: higher-than-projected outlays, in particular recession-induced extra spending for social welfare and higher direct income payments for farmers, were largely offset by lower-than-budgeted interest payments, as interest rates fell more steeply than expected. It is also noteworthy that nominal personnel expenditures contracted slightly (Table 11). The overall growth of federal expenditures considerably in excess of that of nominal GDP may give an exaggerated impression of the dynamism of central government spending: if items are taken out which are heavily influenced either by the business cycle or by the tax-collection cycle, such as debt interest payments, cyclically-induced transfers to unemployment insurance and the transfers of the cantons' shares in federal direct taxes (30 per cent), the average growth of the remaining expenditure components was only 3½ per cent in 1993.

Table 11. Central government budget

SF million

	1990		1991		1992		1993		1994	Percentage changes[1]		
	Outturns	Breakdown in %	Initial budget	Outturns	Initial budget	Outturns	Initial budget	Outturns	Initial budget	1992	1993	1994
Total expenditure	31 616	100.0	33 829	35 501	37 117	37 816	39 738	40 600	42 583	6.5	7.4	4.9
Economic classification												
Compensation of employees	4 056	12.8	4 163	4 393	4 547	4 764	4 788	4 748	4 970	8.4	-0.3	4.7
Consumption	5 363	17.0	5 573	5 582	5 689	5 675	5 456	5 359	5 693	1.7	-5.6	6.2
Investment	582	1.8	713	719	854	810	834	934	849	12.7	15.3	-9.1
Interest, loans, acquisition of holdings	2 242	7.1	2 420	2 634	2 784	3 079	4 254	5 053	5 346	16.9	64.1	5.8
Transfers	19 373	61.3	20 960	22 173	23 244	23 488	24 405	24 506	25 725	5.9	4.3	5.0
Total revenue	32 673	100.0	33 902	33 490	35 788	34 953	36 651	32 782	35 609	4.4	-6.2	8.6
Tax revenue	28 815	88.2	29 854	29 169	31 886	30 406	32 344	28 589	31 498	4.2	-6.0	10.2
Direct taxes	12 846	39.3	12 900	12 888	14 750	14 269	13 850	11 993	14 150	10.7	-16.0	18.0
Indirect taxes	15 969	48.9	16 954	16 281	17 136	16 137	18 494	16 596	17 348	-0.9	2.8	4.5
Other revenue	3 858	11.8	4 048	4 321	3 902	4 547	4 307	4 193	4 111	5.2	-7.8	-2.0
Balance	+1 057		+73	-2 011	-1 329	-2 863	-3 087	-7 818	-6 974			
As a percentage of GDP	+0.3		+0.0	-0.6	-0.4	-0.8	-0.9	-2.3	-2.0			

1. For 1992 and 1993: outturn on outturn of previous period; for 1994: initial budget on outturn for 1993.
Source: Budget of the Swiss Confederation.

However, overly-optimistic macroeconomic projections contributed to a huge gap between realised and expected revenues: instead of the hoped-for increase, total federal revenues fell by 6¼ per cent in 1993. The biggest absolute revenue shortfall was recorded for the tax on capital income (*impôt anticipé*), which is subject to particular forecast uncertainty as it is the difference between gross receipts from withholding tax on interest and dividend income and partial reimbursement of earlier tax payments. Lower net revenues from this tax were largely due to the unexpectedly pronounced fall in interest rates. The lower-than-projected income from turnover tax on goods (*impôt sur le chiffre d'affaires*), which accounts for one-third of federal fiscal revenues and is the most important component of these revenues, was a clear reflection of the delayed economic recovery and especially of the persisting weakness of investment demand.[34] Altogether, the Confederation closed its accounts with a deficit of SF 7.8 billion in 1993, SF 4.7 billion more than budgeted.[35] Hence, the federal government, which only accounts for roughly one-third of general government revenues and expenditures, now contributes more than one-half to the overall deficit.

The 1994 government budgets

Based on the government's projection of 1 per cent real growth and 2½ per cent inflation, the combined deficit of Confederation, cantons and communes (on the definition of the "Statistique financière révisée") is expected to stabilise at SF 16 billion in 1994, which implies a fall in the deficit/GDP ratio to about 4½ per cent. A deficit reduction of SF 1 billion is projected to be brought about by the Confederation, while cantons and communes are budgeting a further deterioration in their finances. Estimates of cyclically-adjusted budget balances suggest a cut in the structural general government deficit by ½ per cent of GDP in 1994, as a consequence of fiscal retrenchment mainly at the level of cantons and, to a lesser extent, of communes. The federal government is estimated to provide some small discretionary stimulus to the economy.

Compared with the outturns of 1993, the budgeted growth of federal expenditures will decelerate from 7.4 per cent in 1993 to 4.9 per cent in 1994, reflecting favourable effects from improving activity and lower inflation as well as spending restraint across a broad range of items. The projected fall in federal investment expenditures (in a narrow sense) by as much as 9.1 per cent seems

61

striking, but the weight of this component in total expenditures only amounts to 2 per cent.

Growth of federal revenues is expected to outstrip that of expenditures by a large margin,[36] rising by 8.6 per cent in 1994, after the fall by 6.2 per cent in 1993. This is to a large measure the result of rapidly growing direct taxes – by a projected 18 per cent in 1994 – as a consequence of the systematic buoyancy of direct federal tax revenues in even years.[37] Indirect tax revenues are forecast only to increase moderately, reflecting the expected mildness of the economic upswing.

The medium-term financial plan of the Confederation

In accordance with practice in preceding years, the Federal Council prepared a medium-term financial plan in combination with the 1994 budget. The purpose of this exercise is to identify potential future financial constraints at as early a stage as possible. The current plan covers the period from 1995 to 1997 and is based on the assumptions of an average annual growth rate of 2 per cent for real output – which equals the long-term average – and of a $2^{1}/_{2}$ per cent inflation rate.[38] On the basis of current economic policies, it is projected that expenditures will grow on average by 5.5 per cent per year and revenues by 3.1 per cent, but due to the time profile of financial flows, deficits would broadly stabilise in the next two years at the level budgeted for 1994, before edging up in 1997 (Table 12). As a ratio of GDP, the deficit would hover around 2 per cent during 1995-97, in contrast to the government's aim of a balanced budget in the medium term. Moreover, with expenditures projected to grow on average somewhat faster than GDP, the federal expenditure/GDP ratio would continue to stay above the 12 per cent mark, thereby distinctly deviating from the Federal Council's 10 per cent norm.

A comparison of current projections with those of the preceding two medium-term plans reveals a considerable slowdown of expenditure growth. This not only reflects the improved cyclical outlook, but also the effect of fiscal redressment, especially the federal government's second savings package ("deuxième programme d'économies") of October 1993, which by now has been adopted by the Parliament (in a slightly modified form). This programme consists almost exclusively of nineteen selected measures to curtail spending, in contrast to the across-the-board linear expenditure cuts of the preceding fiscal

Table 12.   **Financial outlook of the Confederation, 1995-97**

SF million and percentages

	Budget	Outlook			Growth rate annual average	Structure	
	1994	1995	1996	1997	1993-1997	1994	1997
Total expenditure	42 583	44 481	46 670	49 150	5.5	100.0	100.0
Current expenditure	35 837	38 447	41 251	43 474	5.9	84.2	88.5
Total investment[1]	6 746	6 034	5 415	5 676	2.5	15.8	11.5
Direct expenditure	14 332	15 670	16 352	17 204	4.8	33.7	35.0
Transfers	28 251	28 811	30 318	31 946	5.8	66.3	65.0
Total revenues	35 609	37 420	40 130	41 480	3.1	100.0	100.0
Tax revenues	31 498	32 688	35 196	36 428	3.0	88.5	87.8
Direct taxes	14 150	14 200	15 925	16 150	3.9	39.7	38.9
Indirect taxes	17 348	18 488	19 271	20 278	2.3	48.7	48.9
Non-tax revenues	4 111	4 732	4 934	5 052	4.1	11.5	12.2
Balance	–6 974	–7 061	–6 540	–7 670			

1.   Direct expenditure and contribution to investments.
Source: Financial outlook of the Confederation from October 1993.

programme.[39] Starting in 1995, the measures will be introduced stepwise, and will eventually result in annual savings of SF 1 to 1½ billion during 1995 to 1997.

However, projections of revenue growth have also been revised downwards, from an average annual rate of 5½ per cent of the previous medium-term financial plan to the current 3 per cent, which is partly due to the length of the recession and its lagged effects on federal tax revenues. However, the current plan does not yet take into account the introduction of value-added tax (VAT) as from 1995, which was approved by the Swiss people in late November 1993, after the government's current medium-term plan had been established. The extra revenues from VAT are estimated at SF 900 million in 1995 and are projected to grow to SF 1½ billion *per annum* in the following years. However, recently updated projections of the Confederation which include VAT revenues show actual deficits of SF 6 to 7½ billion and structural deficits of more than SF 4 billion in 1995 and 1996, which the Federal Council deems intolerable. It has therefore been decided to work out a third budget consolidation programme this year, which aims at limiting the growth of expenditures to 2 per cent in 1995.

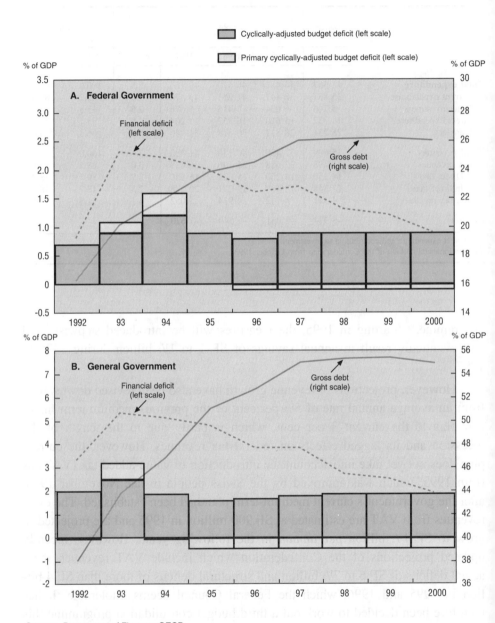

Diagram 19. **MEDIUM-TERM FISCAL PROJECTIONS**
% of GDP

☐ Cyclically-adjusted budget deficit (left scale)

☐ Primary cyclically-adjusted budget deficit (left scale)

A. Federal Government

Financial deficit (left scale)

Gross debt (right scale)

B. General Government

Financial deficit (left scale)

Gross debt (right scale)

Source: Department of Finance; OECD.

Is the current setting of fiscal policy sustainable?

The deterioration in government finances in recent years raises the question of whether the fiscal consolidation measures taken to date will be sufficient to halt the rise in the public debt-GDP ratio in the medium term. To analyse this question, the Secretariat has constructed a baseline scenario through to the year 2000, based on official projections and assumptions.[40] This scenario results in gross-general-government debt rising from about 44 per cent of GDP in 1993 to a peak of 55 per cent of GDP towards the end of the decade. Federal government debt peaks at 26 per cent of GDP at around the same time (Diagram 19), suggesting that – *ceteris paribus* – the recent measures taken to reduce the budget deficit, including the introduction of VAT, should be sufficient to stabilise the debt-GDP ratio in the medium-term.

Fiscal sustainability projections are inevitably sensitive to assumptions about real interest rates and growth. On the official assumptions, a zero primary cyclically-adjusted budget balance (PCAB) is required to stabilise the debt-GDP ratio.[41] If instead it is assumed that real interest rates were 1 percentage point higher than growth starting from the year 2000, a primary structural surplus of ½ per cent of GDP would be required to stabilise general government gross debt at around 55 per cent of GDP. The PCAB already reaches the level required to stabilise the gross debt-GDP ratio in 1994 on the basis of the official assumptions and two years later on the alternative assumption. Provided that the structural component is indeed no more than 40 per cent of this year's general government budget deficit and that the primary structural budget balance of general government can be held to the projected levels, Swiss fiscal policy appears to be sustainable. Such calculations are, however, subject to uncertainty. Since, in addition, mere stabilisation of the debt ratio may not be regarded as a sufficiently ambitious aim for fiscal policy, it would be prudent for the authorities to take further steps towards fiscal consolidation.

III.   Progress in structural reform

Introduction

The government's policy to step up Switzerland's participation in the process of European integration and thereby promote structural reform was dealt a hard blow when Swiss voters decided in the referendum of 6 December 1992 not to ratify the European Economic Area (EEA) Agreement. In order not to lose the momentum behind the efforts to prepare for the EEA and to minimise the potential damage from non-participation in the Agreement – including increased diversion of investment to the EC, especially after its enlargement in January 1995 –, the authorities prepared measures to "revitalise" the Swiss economy. Immediately after the negative referendum a first package of revitalisation measures was adopted by the Swiss government. This revitalisation programme includes measures to liberalise domestic markets – in particular, competition law is to be reformed –, the labour market and public procurement. Simultaneously Switzerland is improving the compatibility of its legislation with EC legislation through the Swisslex programme. This move towards higher "euro-compatibility" covers especially insurance, banking, transport and other legislation. Its aim is to increase the efficiency of the revitalisation programme and to create a basis for improved integration with the EC. After the negative vote on the EEA, the fourth attempt to introduce VAT was made and eventually approved by the people in November 1993. Other current structural policy measures address the provision of infrastructure services, agriculture, social security and public finance. These reform efforts are sketched out below.

The reform of turnover tax

Apart from raising additional federal revenues, the replacement of the antiquated turnover tax by a modern value-added tax is a principal step – advocated by the OECD on many previous occasions – towards a more rational tax system.[42] The current retail sales tax is levied only on goods[43] and with a rate of 6.2 per cent – one of the lowest sales tax rates in the OECD – results in a very low share of indirect taxes in total tax revenues. The present exclusion of services and energy from turnover taxation not only narrows the tax base, but also implies a distortionary effect on resource allocation. But probably the most important drawback of the present retail sales tax is that it is levied not only on consumer goods but also on investment goods and intermediate inputs, a feature usually referred to as the hidden tax (*"taxe occulte"*). The hidden tax thus is likely to have a harmful effect on investment and on international competitiveness in both export and domestic markets. The fact that the turnover tax on investment and intermediate inputs earns about one-half of the total revenues from this tax suggests that the magnitude of this effect is non-negligible, and explains why this important source of federal revenue is subject to relatively strong cyclical fluctuations.

Because of the disadvantages of the old turnover tax, several attempts had been made to replace it by VAT. But in Switzerland, the final say on tax matters lies with the voters: top rates of main federal taxes can be changed, and new taxes introduced, only by constitutional amendment following a compulsory referendum. The three referenda held on VAT in 1977, 1979 and 1991 ended with the rejection of the government's proposals by the Swiss people. However, in the fourth referendum on 28 November 1993, a majority voted not only in favour of VAT, but also opted for setting the VAT rate at 6.5 per cent instead of the current 6.2 per cent for turnover tax; along with their approval of VAT, Swiss voters also endorsed the prolongation of the Confederation's right to raise the federal direct tax – which expired at the end of 1994 – to the year 2006. A constitutional amendment, following a compulsory referendum, will be required in order to levy the federal direct tax and the value-added tax after the year 2006. In addition, voters gave the government authority to raise the VAT rate by 1 percentage point in the future to help finance the old-age insurance scheme. To compensate for a possible regressive income effect of VAT, it has been decided to use 5 per cent of the VAT revenues for cuts in the health insurance premium for lower income groups during a transitional period of five years. The new system is expected to go into effect on 1 January 1995, after details of its implementation have been worked out.

Technical issues which are currently being addressed by the Swiss authorities relate to the exact list of goods and services which will either be exempted from VAT (among them certain services of a medical, cultural or educational nature, specific banking services and insurance premia) or will be subject to a preferential rate of 2.0 per cent (basic goods). The issue of the taxation of bank customers domiciled outside Switzerland (the "export" of banking services) gained particular prominence in the current debate. Another subject of discussion is the suggestion by entrepreneurs' associations to advance to mid-1994 the deductibility from tax liabilities of taxes paid on investment goods offered by VAT in order to avoid large scale deferral of business investment into 1995 when the *"taxe occulte"* will no longer be levied. However, selective measures of this kind would risk serious consequences for federal revenues in 1994.

Revitalisation of the economy and Swisslex

The work on structural reform launched after the people and the cantons rejected the European Economic Area (EEA) Agreement on 6 December 1992 has progressed. Parliament has approved a number of changes in Swiss legislation which would have been necessary had Switzerland participated in the EEA; these changes are known as Swisslex. These reforms are wide-ranging, including, for example, regulations on animal epidemics, trade in processed agricultural products, producer liability and workers' rights to information and consultation within an enterprise.[44] One of the main reasons for implementing these reforms, despite the rejection of EEA membership, is to harmonise certain Swiss laws and standards with those of the EC.

Moreover, the Federal Council has embarked on a comprehensive programme of structural reforms known as "revitalisation" or "regeneration" of the Swiss economy. These reforms aim at increasing competition, simplifying government administrative procedures and improving the efficiency of the public sector. The first package of 22 measures, which the Federal Council announced on 23 February 1993, covers five main areas:

- competition policy;
- the domestic market;
- the labour market;
- education policy;
- speeding up certain administrative procedures.

Most of these measures will require legislative changes.[45]

Competition policy and the liberalisation of the domestic market are the two essential points of the revitalisation programme, entailing:

- a complete revision of cartel law. For constitutional reasons, the system will still be based on the abuse principle. Nevertheless, the new law will be stricter and clearer as a result of the introduction of harm presumption clauses for cartels directly or indirectly setting prices, restricting the volume of goods and services for purchase or supply, or dividing up the market on a territorial basis. New provisions will also be introduced for abuses of a dominant position and for a preliminary control on mergers. Administrative procedures are also to be simplified. A new Federal Competition Office will be set up to conduct investigations and to run the secretariat of a council of independent experts. It is also planned to send the explanatory message to Parliament during the second half of this year and to amend the law on unfair competition in the near future;
- the adoption of a federal law which would remove technical impediments to trade. This law will be outlined in a message to be sent to Parliament at the end of this year. Its primary aim is to eliminate technical import barriers and to open markets to competition which are protected by specifically Swiss technical standards;
- the adoption of a framework law on the Swiss domestic market to combat public regulations, notably at canton and commune level, that are protectionist, with a view to strengthening the freedom of trade and industry enshrined in the Federal Constitution. This law will promote free trade in goods and services and the free movement of labour, principally by providing for non-discriminatory access to public contracts and mutual recognition of cantonal diplomas. Henceforth, the domestic market will be governed by the "Cassis de Dijon" principle, which guarantees, for all forms of economic activity, the mutual recognition of cantonal and communal regulations and permits obtained at the place of origin. The preliminary draft law of 21 January 1994 provides for the mutual recognition of vocational qualifications and cantonal diplomas, and obliges cantons and communes to advertise public contracts in an official publication. A separate law now being drawn up will liberalise public tendering procedures at the federal level – a consequence of the new GATT code for public contracts.

The revision of the cartel law and the adoption of the laws removing technical impediments to trade in the Swiss domestic market and liberalising public tendering procedures will also be approved by the government and sent to the Parliament before the end of the year.

Among the other important reforms being drawn up or going through Parliament are:

- the conversion of technical, commercial and arts-oriented schools into higher-level schools (Hautes écoles spécialisées) aimed at better integrating applied research, theoretical training and work experience;
- partial revision of the law on land use, primarily with a view to simplifying and speeding up administrative and legal procedures; and
- amendment of the law on the residence and establishment of foreigners with a view to adjusting the status of seasonal workers to that of foreign short-time workers in the EC legislation.

The revitalisation measures that have already been introduced concern certain aspects of the labour market and minor regulations that were within the competence of the federal government. For example, the requirement that indigenous workers must be given priority for jobs was abolished on 1 May 1993 for highly-skilled specialists and managers. On 1 November 1993, the status of frontier workers was improved by granting, after five years, extended occupational and geographical mobility to workers who reside outside Switzerland.

A second global package of reforms within the scope of the revitalisation programme was adopted in June 1994 by the Swiss Federal Council. This new package focuses on infrastructure (mainly reorganisation of the postal services, of the railway and the telecommunications sectors), social security, agricultural policy in the aftermath of the GATT agreement of 15 December 1993 and public finance. Concerning the latter, the Swiss authorities intend to reduce the budget deficit (*via* a fiscal consolidation programme and a review of transfers), and to improve corporate taxation: reducing double taxation of profits, lowering stamp duty on share issues, and introducing a proportional rate of profits tax.

Infrastructure

Switzerland has extensive, high-quality infrastructure at all levels, which besides meeting local and regional needs also carries a large amount of international traffic. The internationalisation of economic activity and the growth of international competition pose a two-fold challenge to Switzerland. First, structural developments call for renewed investment to keep abreast of recent technical and technological advances, especially in communications and transport. It is for this reason that the Swiss Confederation is planning, like Germany, to reorganise and make more autonomous the major federal public corporations, the federal railways (CFF) and the PTT, with a view to enabling them better to withstand domestic and foreign competition, without, however, planning to privatise them completely. However, as a result of the new, more restrictive delimitation of the activity of public monopolies, new opportunities for the private sector are expected to emerge, with additional investment and a reinforcement of innovative capabilities. Second, it is necessary to take appropriate account of the European Union's concerns about passenger and freight transit within an increasingly integrated Europe. For example, the motorway network is already very extensive and connected to those of neighbouring countries. As for rail traffic, major projects are in place, in particular the upgrading of parts of the "Rail 2000" network and the construction of new Alpine rail links.

The network of national roads, most of which was designed at the beginning of the 1960s, is very dense in relation to the size of the country and its population. The Federal Council's fourth long-term construction programme, which was adopted in 1992, provides for the completion of the last fifth of the network over the next fifteen years. The estimated cost per kilometre is very high owing to construction standards that are becoming more complex all the time, and the need to meet environmental requirements. The programme will be financed out of fuel taxes, which rose by 20 centimes per litre last year. Since construction of the first section of motorway began in the early 1960s, the rate of car ownership has increased four-fold, from 9.3 to less than two persons per car. As a result, some very busy sections of the network are prone to bottlenecks, especially during the holiday period when the network also has to carry transit traffic. The expansion of the road network has brought it into direct competition with the large rail network, which the authorities, however, want to make more attractive, primarily for environmental reasons.

The aim of the "Rail 2000" investment programme, the initial project of which dates from 1985, is to upgrade the entire rail network with a view to increasing train speeds and improving connections. To this end, it is planned, in addition to upgrading parts of existing lines, to build new lines and adapt ancillary infrastructure (technical services, stations, etc.) to new requirements. Because of funding problems, the initial project has undergone modifications, though they should not affect the basic objectives. The first stage of the project, now under way, will cost about SF 7 billion. The financial feasibility study has not ruled out the possibility of financial losses. However, this possibility is offset in the eyes of the government by the environmental benefits of the project (in terms of improved safety, reduced noise and air pollution, and the amount of land taken up) and its impact on mobility (for example, complementarity with the road network).

The Alpine rail project provides essentially for the construction of two tunnels and connecting rail links.[46] The project was approved by popular vote on 27 September 1992. Its purpose is to increase transport capacity on the north-south axis, and in particular to create the infrastructure for the transport by rail of transit freight and truck traffic. A quarter of the immediate cost of the project is being funded out of fuel taxes, the remainder by public loans to the two owners, the CFF and the private rail company BLS (Berne-Lotschberg-Simplon). According-ing to the feasibility and profitability studies that have been carried out, the loans could be repaid in 60 years out of user revenues.

One of the main aims of the project is to reduce the damage caused to the environment by road traffic. Indeed, it was primarily for this reason that, during the negotiations on transit traffic with the EC, Switzerland wanted to ban trucks weighing more than 28 tonnes overall. The agreement concluded allows fifty 40-tonne lorries per day to travel through Switzerland but only in exceptional circumstances (for example, for the transport of perishable goods) and if rail capacity for transporting lorries is unavailable. The uncertainty surrounding the economic and financial profitability of the Alpine links is due primarily to the fact that it is not known how much road transport will actually switch to rail. The constitutional initiative adopted in February 1994 by the people and cantons on the "protection of the Alpine regions against transit traffic" obliges the govern-ment to transfer transit freight traffic from the roads to rail within ten years and prohibits any expansion of the infrastructure for transit road traffic. Parliament adopted the law on transit routes in June 1994. This law defines four alpine routes (Gotthard, San Bernardino, Grand St. Bernhard and Simplon) and freezes road transport capacity at the level of February 1994. The transfer from road to rail transit is to be achieved by market instruments and by an improvement in rail transport services for lorries. These changes in the conditions for transit traffic are in accordance with the obligations of the agreement reached with the EC.

Social security

Unemployment insurance

At the end of the 1980s, the revenue surpluses in the unemployment insurance scheme, which largely reflected the fall in unemployment, gave rise to a first revision of the scheme. The contribution rate – of which employers and employees each pay one-half – was lowered from 0.6 per cent of gross wages (below an indexed ceiling)[47] to 0.4 per cent in 1990. The reserves built up prior to 1991 contributed to the funding of the SF 2.7 billion excess in expenditure in 1992, the number of jobless having risen fivefold compared with 1990. Although the contribution rate was increased to 2 per cent from 1 January 1993 – the maximum legal level – this was not sufficient to meet the insurance scheme's current borrowing requirement. The scheme recorded a SF 2.3 billion deficit in 1993 which was financed by loans from the Confederation and cantons.

Under the ongoing revision of the legislation on unemployment insurance, the Federal Council proposes to increase the maximum contribution rate it can impose to 3 per cent and to raise the ceiling on the gross wage liable to contributions two-and-a-half-fold. On the benefits side, the declining scale – abolished on 1 January 1993 – is to be reintroduced for certain categories of jobless, the concept of acceptable work is to be more broadly defined and active measures to prevent and curb unemployment are to be reinforced, especially in the areas of training, support for self-employment and job-seeking. The revised legislation is expected to retain the present maximum period of compensation, which was lengthened on 1 April 1993 from 300 to 400 days; this increase in benefits was enacted by urgent federal government legislation and approved by referendum on 26 September 1993. Lastly, it is proposed to extend the waiting period for those leaving school and higher education from 20 days to 6 months. These changes in unemployment insurance curtail certain benefits which were increased at a time when unemployment was very low, but also require businesses and wage-earners to pay higher contributions. This compromise ensures a minimum level of funding of benefits, the aim being not to jeopardise medium-term fiscal consolidation. The changes are scheduled to come into force in the second half of 1995, subject to the legislation being adopted rapidly by Parliament, and depending also on the outcome of a referendum which might be called for by employers and/or unions, for opposite reasons.

Old-age insurance

The reforms proposed as part of the tenth revision of the old-age and survivors' insurance scheme (AVS), which were submitted by the Federal Council in March 1990, have since been the subject of regular discussion by Parliament. One of the stumbling blocks concerns the financing of the significant increases in benefits which are proposed: measures to establish equal entitlements for men and women – notably if the retirement age for men as an option were to be lowered by one year to 64 (while for women it were raised from 62 to 64); and if account were to be taken of the years that women spend raising their children. Further unresolved issues are the improvement in benefits for the disabled, the method of calculating pensions, the introduction of early retirement and the replacement of benefits paid to those with insufficient contributions to be entitled to the minimum old-age pension by supplementary benefits (related to needs). The overall cost of the reform is estimated to be in the region of SF 500 to 800 million, depending on the assumptions made. Acceptance of these improvements in benefits will hasten an in-depth reform in funding, the financial equilibrium of the insurance system being guaranteed, under present conditions, only until the end of the century. The dependency ratio is constantly increasing and can even be expected to accelerate towards the year 2005. It follows either that the contribution rate, which is at present 8.4 per cent of the gross wage, will have to be revised upwards in the course of the coming ten years, or else the VAT rate will have to be increased by a maximum of 1 percentage point, in accordance with the provisions constitutionally voted last year.

Sickness insurance

The ratio of health spending to GDP in Switzerland is about the OECD average, even though such spending rose by 6 per cent in the 1980s, faster than GDP. Given high relative prices of health care, Swiss households' consumption of health care services is still, in volume terms, below the level "predicted" by

74

the econometrically calculated ratio of health spending to per capita GDP (Diagram 20). However, individuals' insurance premiums have gone up sharply, partly because of the freeze on federal transfers, which remained unchanged for more than a decade, up until 1990. Pending the revision of the sickness insurance law, the government has been using emergency federal orders (AFU) to curb the growth of health spending. The first of these froze fee charges until end-1992 and put a 10 per cent limit on the increase in insurance premiums. On 1 January 1993, another AFU introduced a contribution to hospitalisation costs of SF 10 per day and limited the services reimbursed by sickness funds to compulsory services. When a single premium for each sickness fund was brought in at cantonal level, this necessitated a third AFU and also the introduction of a system of risk compensation between funds. Treating the symptoms in this way can have only a limited and short-term effect on health spending which is determined by decisions taken in the private sector (patients, doctors), and independently by the cantons where hospitals are concerned.

The new law on sickness insurance, voted by Parliament in April, introduces compulsory insurance and complete freedom of movement between sickness

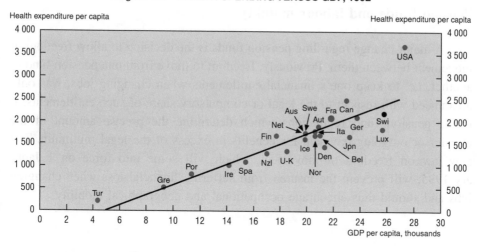

Diagram 20. **HEALTH SPENDING VERSUS GDP, 1992**

Note: Data shown are PPPs in US dollars, converted to a price level OECD = 100.
Source: OECD, *Purchasing Power Parities and Real Expenditures,* and *OECD Health Systems Facts and Trends.*

75

funds. As was recommended in the recent report by the Cartel Commission (1993), it seeks to stimulate competition by forbidding associations and groups providing services and insurance from claiming an exclusive right to conclude fee agreements. This provision establishes a legal basis for new forms of health care and insurance organisation, such as the Health Maintenance Organisation (HMO) which were authorised to operate on a temporary basis for five years on 1 January 1990. The list of services reimbursed by the sickness funds has also been extended, in particular by the inclusion of care provided outside hospitals, in the home and in community health centres, the object being to put all forms of health care on the same footing. The idea that patients should contribute to hospital costs has been maintained in the form of a 10 per cent share in costs in excess of a given allowance up to a ceiling set by the government. A number of exceptional cost-control measures are planned, including the application of budget appropriation techniques for hospitals and the freezing of fees in the event of steep increases. The new law should come into force on 1 January 1996, but the chances of it being put to a referendum cannot be ruled out. In conjunction with the revision of the sickness insurance system, a maternity insurance scheme is also in preparation which would be financed from social insurance contributions.

Pension funds and labour mobility

A major change regarding pension funds is the decision to allow freedom of movement between them. Previously, freedom to move from one pension fund to another, i.e. to keep one's financial entitlements when changing jobs, was only guaranteed with respect to the legal or compulsory share of such entitlements. It is the pension fund regulations which determine the precise amount of the transfer or outgoing payment for benefits in excess of the legal minimum. The new law on freedom of movement, which will come into force on 1 January 1995, will prevent the insured from suffering financial loss when changing jobs and should thus encourage occupational and geographical mobility.

IV.   Selected issues in construction, housing and land use

Introduction

Switzerland is a well-off country that enjoys a magnificent natural landscape. Over many decades, the Swiss have, quite reasonably, sought to preserve and to enhance their living environment. They have done so through the adoption of zoning restrictions and building codes. These and other factors – notably weak enforcement of competition law in construction and related sectors and the regulation of construction trades – have combined to inflate construction costs and land prices and to dampen the rate of new construction. Taken together, these characteristics have acted to lift housing costs.

Recently, the Swiss authorities have taken measures to increase the rate of owner occupancy (which is one of the lowest in the OECD area) and to promote new residential construction. During the last three years, the Swiss authorities have increased their efforts to promote new residential construction within the existing housing legislation as well as taken measures to increase the rate of owner occupancy through changes to occupational pension regulations which come into effect next year. This chapter examines the general policy framework bearing on construction and land use in Switzerland. It then describes and evaluates other aspects of housing policy, including tenant protection regulation and programmes designed to promote owner-occupancy and new home construction. Finally, it evaluates the combined impacts of these policies with respect to Switzerland's numerous objectives in the areas of housing and land use.

Construction prices and costs

The construction sector has an important effect on the performance of the Swiss economy because of its size and links to other sectors. It accounts for a

77

Box 1. The dimensions of the construction sector

Construction expenditure accounts for around 17 per cent of GDP in Switzerland, second only to Japan in the OECD area as a proportion of GDP (Table 13); expressed in purchasing power parities (PPPs), construction expenditure per head is the highest in the OECD (see Box 2). As in other countries, the construction sector is highly cyclical, rising in proportion to GDP during expansions and falling during economic downturns. This tendency was particularly marked in Switzerland during the 1970s when construction contracted sharply following the first oil price shock. Construction has since recovered somewhat and, abstracting from cyclical variations, has remained stable as a proportion of GDP. In contrast, there has been a trend decline in construction relative to GDP in most other European countries.

Around two-thirds of total investment expenditure in Switzerland is on construction (see Table 13). This proportion is also one of the highest in the OECD and, in particular, is well above the levels observed in most other European countries. Once again, there has been a trend decline in this ratio in most other countries but not in Switzerland.

Table 13.   **Total construction expenditure**

Current prices

	1970-74		1975-79		1980-84		1985-89		1990-92	
	(1)	(2)	(1)	(2)	(1)	(2)	(1)	(2)	(1)	(2)
Switzerland	18.7	65.1	14.5	66.8	16.2	69.0	16.7	65.4	16.8	66.1
Austria	15.4	54.8	14.3	55.1	12.6	53.1	11.9	51.2	13.2	52.0
Belgium	n.a.	n.a.	14.1	64.9	10.8	60.6	8.8	52.1	n.a.	n.a.
Denmark	16.7	68.3	13.9	64.0	9.8	58.5	10.6	55.4	8.8	53.8
France	15.5	62.2	14.5	62.7	12.8	60.2	11.2	55.6	11.4	55.0
Germany	15.7	64.3	12.6	61.2	12.9	61.3	11.0	56.0	11.6	54.6
Japan	21.1	60.2	20.7	66.4	19.2	65.0	17.3	60.0	19.0	60.3
Netherlands	15.2	62.0	13.0	60.9	11.9	60.7	10.9	52.4	10.7	52.1
Norway	16.8	58.4	20.8	62.4	17.3	66.7	18.7	69.4	n.a.	n.a.
Spain	16.1	62.5	15.5	65.1	14.1	66.8	13.6	64.1	16.0	68.2
United Kingdom	10.6	54.8	10.2	53.7	8.9	53.6	9.8	53.4	9.5	55.1
United States	11.5	72.9	11.3	67.4	11.1	65.0	10.4	64.4	8.5	63.1

1.   As percentage of GDP.
2.   As percentage of total fixed investment.
Source: OECD, National Accounts.

(continued on next page)

(continued)

Construction expenditure can be divided into three main categories – residential; non-residential structures; and public works. The first two categories are mainly under-taken for the private sector while the latter category, which principally consists of infrastructure investment, is primarily for the government; compared with most other OECD countries, residential construction for government (*i.e.* social housing) appears to be small.[48] Residential construction accounts for 35 per cent of total construction expen-diture, non-residential construction for a further 46 per cent (of which approximately two-thirds is private sector) and public works for the remaining 19 per cent. Government construction expenditure is largely attributable to lower levels of government: the federal government, cantons and local government, respectively, accounted for 20 per cent, 32 per cent and 48 per cent of government construction expenditure in 1993.[49]

Employment in the construction sector[50] and in the industries[51] providing intermedi-ate inputs directly to it is estimated by the Société Suisse des Entrepreneurs (SSE) to have been 19 per cent of total employment in 1991, while construction expenditure accounted for 16.9 per cent of GDP in that year. On a narrow definition of construction (*i.e.* exclud-ing all intermediate inputs), the most recent federal businesses survey (for the month of September 1991) shows that employment was 11.4 per cent of total employment.[52]

large proportion of GDP, is the largest category of gross investment and is a major input into other sectors (see Box 1).

There are concerns that the efficiency of this and related sectors is compro-mised by anti-competitive practices and government regulations. Among the anti-competitive practices are the activities of cartels and the use of industry norms and of government procurement policies to restrict competition. This section reviews these practices and regulations and describes reforms presently being considered in this sector.

Construction prices – an international comparison

Construction prices in Switzerland expressed in PPP terms are (based on data for 1990) around one-third higher than the average for OECD countries and are only exceeded by those in Sweden (Table 14).[53] Within this total, both residential and non-residential building prices are almost 40 per cent above the OECD average while the price for public works is approximately one-quarter higher than the OECD average.

Table 14. Comparative dollar price levels in construction 1990

OECD = 100[1]

	Switzerland	Austria	Denmark	European Union	France	Germany	Japan	Spain	Sweden	United Kingdom	United States
Gross rent and water charges	152	90	112	82	89	124	142	64	130	72	112
Construction	134	106	128	104	94	118	130	91	152	117	79
Residential buildings	137	122	162	109	98	138	133	82	159	109	79
Non residential buildings	139	107	135	107	104	114	112	83	158	125	81
Civil engineering works	124	80	85	92	75	93	145	102	134	118	81
Gross domestic product	140	109	134	104	107	114	119	95	139	95	88

1. Comparative price levels are defined as the ratios of purchasing power parities to exchange rates. They indicate for a given aggregate the number of units of the common currency needed to buy the same volume of the aggregate in each country.

Source: OECD, Purchasing Power Parities and Real Expenditures, Paris, 1992.

While Swiss construction prices are certainly high, they are not unusually so in relation to other prices in Switzerland – in PPP terms, Swiss output prices are some 40 per cent above the average for OECD countries and the highest in the OECD area. Moreover, at least in the case of residential construction,[54] Swiss prices have fallen markedly relative to output prices since the first oil price shock in the 1970s (Diagram 21).[55] This is in marked contrast to developments in most other countries.

Diagram 21. **RELATIVE PRICE OF RESIDENTIAL CONSTRUCTION**

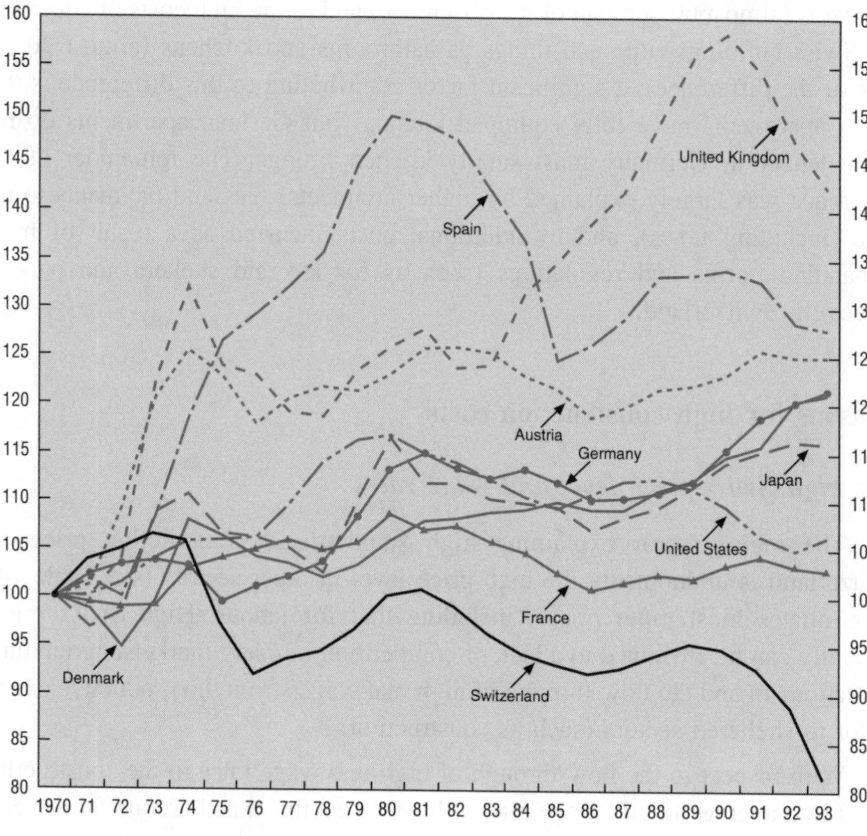

Source: OECD, *Annual National Accounts.*

Construction costs

Construction costs, which reflect not only the standardised construction prices just discussed but also differences in specifications and in prices for materials, appear to be considerably higher than in other countries. It was found in a recent study that construction costs for a representative apartment building were 29 per cent higher in Switzerland than in Germany;[56] in view of the high standardised residential construction prices in Germany, these construction costs are likely to be very high indeed relative to those in most other OECD countries. Moreover, this difference was found despite prices for comparable elements of the buildings taken in isolation being lower in Switzerland.[57] Higher Swiss construction costs were mainly attributable to more demanding construction standards (almost 60 per cent of the difference) and to the high costs of equipping the Swiss building with such things as bathrooms and kitchens (almost 20 per cent of the difference); a significant factor contributing to this difference is that Swiss apartments have fully equipped kitchens but German apartments do not – the tenant in Germany must supply kitchen fittings. The remainder of the difference was largely explained by higher architects' fees and payments to the state (including taxes), and by additional costs incurred as a result of more demanding norms and regulations (such as for air raid shelters and parking spaces) in Switzerland.

Reasons for high construction costs

The high Swiss price level and wage rates

The major factor explaining high standardised construction prices in Switzerland is undoubtedly the high price level in other sectors (see Table 14). This inflates most input prices, including that for labour. High Swiss prices generally can be attributed to a lack of competition in many markets, agricultural protectionism and the flow-through of high real wages from the productive export sector to sheltered sectors (such as construction).[58]

With respect to the flow-through of high real wage rates to the construction sector, the average hourly wage rate in this sector[59] fluctuated around 94 per cent of the national average (Diagram 22) over most of the 1980s even though labour productivity (per employee) was considerably lower: 80 per cent of the national

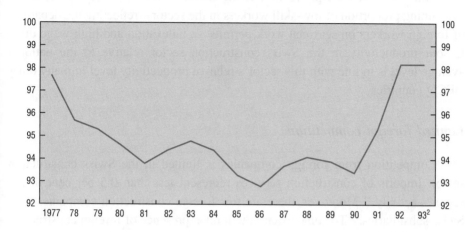

Diagram 22. **AVERAGE WAGE RATES IN CONSTRUCTION**[1]

National average = 100

1. Hourly.
2. Estimation.
Source: Office fédéral de l'industrie, des arts et métiers et du travail.

Table 15. **Value-added and employment in the construction sector**

Per cent

	1985			1990		
	Value-added share	Employment share	Relative productivity	Valued-added share	Employment share	Relative productivity
Switzerland	7.4	9.3	80	8.1	9.6	84
Austria[1]	6.6	7.6	87	7.0	7.7	91
Belgium	5.2	6.1	86	5.4	6.7	81
Denmark	5.0	6.7	75	5.2	6.4	82
Finland	6.8	7.9	86	8.5	9.1	94
France	5.2	7.1	73	5.0	7.2	69
Germany	5.2	7.0	74	5.3	6.7	78
Italy	6.3	7.3	86	5.8	7.0	84
Japan	7.9	9.0	88	9.9	9.2	108
Netherlands[2]	5.0	7.6	66	5.4	7.6	71
Norway	5.4	7.6	71	4.4	7.3	61
Spain	6.7	7.0	96	9.1	9.5	96
Sweden	5.9	6.3	94	6.9	6.6	104
United Kingdom	5.2	6.2	84	6.5	6.9	94

1. Employees only.
2. In man-years, for 1987 and 1990.
Source: OECD, *National Accounts,* Office fédéral de la statistique, Compte de production 1985 et 1990.

average in 1985 and 84 per cent in 1990 (Table 15).[60] Construction wage rates have since increased sharply relative to the national average largely as a result of a declining proportion of low-skill workers in the sector – reflecting the departure of foreign workers on seasonal work permits – , indexation and high wage drift. Labour productivity in the Swiss construction sector relative to the national average level is in line with this sector's relative productivity level in many other OECD countries.

Limited foreign competition

Competition from foreign companies is limited in the Swiss construction sector. Imports of construction services represent less than 0.5 per cent of the sector's activity.[61] Moreover, there are few foreign construction companies with Swiss subsidiaries.[62] To some extent, the limited presence of foreign construction companies could reflect the comparatively recent nature of internationalisation in this sector within Europe – this trend really only got underway in the late 1980's. But it may also be due to legal barriers – specifically the Lex Friedrich – to the foreign ownership of real estate in Switzerland.[63] This makes it difficult for foreign construction companies to undertake large projects (such as, for example, constructing an apartment building) as they would normally require the company to own property until they are finished.

Non-competitive government procurement policies

Government procurement policies, essentially at the lower levels of government, also restrict competition, not only from foreign companies, but also from non-local Swiss companies; as government buys one-third of the construction industry's output, these policies have a significant effect on the industry. These policies frequently have little regard for competitive principles. Rather, such policies are often used to pursue such goals as protecting local enterprises and employment, subsidising small and medium enterprises and favouring regional development. At the cantonal level of government, various devices are used to exclude non-local competitors from public contracts. Frequently, these devices involve the imposition of restrictive qualifying conditions for an enterprise to be able to submit a bid. Examples of such conditions include those relating to domicile, the time elapsed since the enterprise was created and membership of certain organisations, such as the local chamber of commerce or a professional association.[64] Other devices to exclude outsiders include the automatic exclusion of the best offer or indeed of all offers below professional associations' reference prices and the abusive use of government charges. Public procurement in around one-half of the cantons is principally guided by non-competitive considerations. Felder *et al.* (1993) estimated that these policies added at least 3.7 per cent to the cost of public purchases in these cantons.[65]

Cartel agreements amongst construction companies also boost the cost of public works. These agreements, which are sometimes made when tenders are called for public works, aim at dividing the work amongst a number of enterprises and fixing in advance the prices submitted to the authorities.

Construction regulations and norms

Construction laws, regulations and norms[66] are clearly necessary to ensure that the enjoyment of an individual's property does not impose unreasonable costs on others and that whatever is constructed will be able to meet certain reasonable performance standards. But there are concerns that construction laws and regulations in Switzerland are too restrictive and have high compliance costs. There also doubts about whether such demanding industry norms are really necessary.

The effect on construction costs of high minimum standards imposed by regulations and laws and by industry norms was highlighted in the comparative study of the costs of constructing similar apartment buildings in Switzerland and Germany. The question arises as to whether the higher standards set in Switzerland are really necessary to meet buyers' requirements.[67] While some aspects of the difference in requirements between the two countries may be justified to meet differences in physical conditions and community preferences, there are reasons to suspect that there could be an element of over-specification by the industry. In particular, buyers of construction services do not generally possess the same information as suppliers – they do not know if certain industry norms are really necessary. Similarly, as voters, they are not in a position to judge the merits of building regulations. On the other hand, industry representatives have strong incentives to convince government officials of the need for regulations and laws specifying high minimum standards. The federal government is concerned that regulations and norms may be inflating construction costs unnecessarily and proposes a critical review of these requirements as one of the ways which could lead to lower construction costs.

Construction regulations and laws also inflate construction costs by imposing high compliance costs. These rules vary considerably from one canton and commune to another, increasing costs for those wishing to offer construction and related services (especially architectural and engineering services) in different parts of the country. The rules are also contradictory on occasions; for example, regulations for sound and thermal insulation are often inconsistent with fire safety regulations. And bureaucratic procedures for acquiring the necessary permits from the authorities are long and complicated; and in the case of those relating to land development, they also artificially inflate land values.[68]

Cartels in ancillary industries

Cartels are endemic in the ancillary industries to construction, inflating the prices of building materials and fittings. The Cartels Commission has already investigated the abuse of market power by cartels in the markets for bathroom and kitchen fittings (1968, 1973 and 1991), cables (1977), bricks and stones (1978), wall paper (1981) and cement (1993). And the Commission is presently investigating the markets for sand, gravel and prefabricated concrete.

The extent to which cartels in these industries can inflate prices depends on their coverage and, in particular, the potential for competition from imports. In the case of the cement industry, prices do not seem to have been exorbitant, despite 98 per cent market coverage, because of the potential for import competition. However, the bathroom and kitchen fittings industries have been able to influence prices because they have fixed technical standards which severely restrict imports – so much so that the major supplier of bathroom fittings has nearly 90 per cent of the market. And such standards are sometimes reinforced by government regulations; reinforcement by unofficial rules is, however, more common.

The bathroom and kitchen fittings case highlights the difficulties of disbanding some cartels. The Cartels Commission has found against the industry on numerous occasions, but the cartel remains as strong as ever. This reflects weaknesses in current competition law and in its administration. For a cartel to be ruled illegal, the Cartels Commission must prove that the complainant suffers harm. This is not always easy to demonstrate, especially in view of the Commission's lack of staff.[69] Even after a cartel has been ruled illegal, many years can elapse before it is disbanded because of extensive appeal possibilities and drawn-out administrative procedures. And there is always the possibility that the technical standards which reinforce market power could continue in the absence of the cartel. This must be a particular risk in the bathroom fittings industry where the dominant firm is almost in a monopoly position.[70]

Internal market barriers in ancillary industries

Local-government regulations, frequently concerning technical standards, often present barriers to domestic trade in the ancillary industries. Less subtle are the regulations which discriminate against non-local firms in the installation of kitchens and bathrooms. To be able to connect such fittings to the water supply, it is necessary to have a permit from the local authority. This permit is available for a flat-rate fee which is independent of the number of connections to be made. Thus, it dissuades suppliers from entering a local market on an occasional basis. Regulations of this type are very effective at closing a market to potential competitors.

Organisation

One consequence of the internal market barriers in ancillary industries is that the development of large firms is inhibited. As a result, production in these industries remains artisanal and is poorly co-ordinated. For example, separate artisans install the various parts of a bathroom instead of a single firm installing the whole bathroom. This increases costs considerably.

With respect to the construction industry, a number of organisational features inflate costs (Table 16). These include a lack of co-ordination amongst project partners, little knowledge or interest amongst architects and engineers about how to reduce construction costs and remuneration of these specialists based on project costs; the last problem, however, is shared with many other countries.

Table 16. **List of problems, measures to take and their consequences**

	Problems	Measures	Consequences
Preparation of construction projects	Frequent lack of detailed data about the project and site.	Comprehensive market survey and detailed information to be provided by the client about the project and site.	Possibility of anticipating trends and imbalances between supply and demand.
	Lack of clear objectives on the part of the client.	Client to draw up precise specifications before giving instructions to the architect.	Scope for large but unquantifiable savings.
	Architectural competitions do not give sufficient weight to the financial aspects.	Lay down criteria for evaluating, breaking down and estimating costs of projects by individual elements (and not by volume).	Scope for large, short- and medium-term, unquantifiable, savings.
	Not enough is known about the financial consequences of building design.	Thorough examination of design specifications (size of living area, excavations, etc.).	Scope for large but unquantifiable savings.
Project management	Lack of co-ordination between project partners.	Simplify lists of services requested, and make better use of contractors, know-how.	Scope for large but unquantifiable savings, drawing up simplified lists of services in the long term.
	Cost reductions are not rewarded in payments for services and fees.	Introduction of a performance-related system of payment.	Scope for savings in the medium-term, scale of fees currently being revised.
	Designers do not pay enough attention to keeping costs down.	Make architects and engineers more aware of costs, and provide training in achieving savings in construction.	Long-term strategic effect in technical schools and universities.
Construction techniques	Equipment and equipment standards too costly.	Scrap, reduce or simplify certain equipment.	Potential savings of about 17 per cent, but with some loss of quality.
	Possibilities of standardisation and prefabrication not used sufficiently.	Standardisation is possible, especially for construction components, dimensions and drawings.	Scope for long-term but unquantifiable savings.

Table 16. **List of problems, measures to take and their consequences** *(cont.)*

	Problems	Measures	Consequences
The environment of the construction sector	Lack of competition in some branches of construction.	Increase competition during the design phase, combat cartels and collusive agreements, expand the Swiss domestic market.	Scope for long-term but unquantifiable savings.
	The time required to obtain construction permits is too long.	Closer collaboration between designers and collusive agreements, expand the Swiss domestic market.	Scope for modest savings in the fairly long-term.
	Specifications that tend to push up the cost of construction.	Critical analysis of specifications and identification of conflicting aims.	Scope for large savings, though often they may be in conflict with objectives outside the sphere of construction proper (environmental considerations, civil defence, etc.).
	Lack of co-ordination between specifications for sound-proofing, thermal insulation and fire protection.	Rapid harmonisation of national specifications, better documentation and simplification of calculation methods.	Scope for small savings in the fairly long-term.

Source: Federal Housing Office, "Reducing the costs of housing construction", *Report on Housing*, No. 27, Bern, 1993.

Reforms to reduce construction costs

The policy framework described above is not the only factor underpinning high construction costs and expenditures (see Box 2), but it appears to make a significant contribution. The Swiss authorities have been considering various

---

Box 2. High construction expenditure in Switzerland

Real construction expenditure per capita (converted to dollars at 1990 purchasing power parities (PPPs)) for construction in Switzerland was almost $4 500 in 1990, by far the highest level in the OECD (Diagram 23). To a large extent, this level of expenditure reflects high real incomes. Expenditure on construction appears to rise more than in proportion to incomes and Swiss GDP per capita (converted to dollars at PPP exchange rates) was the second highest (behind the United States) in the OECD. This tendency presumably reflects the priority which households attach to obtaining larger and better quality residences as income permits and community preferences for better infrastructure.

Diagram 23. **PER CAPITA CONSTRUCTION EXPENDITURE AND GDP**
At thousands of 1990 PPP dollars

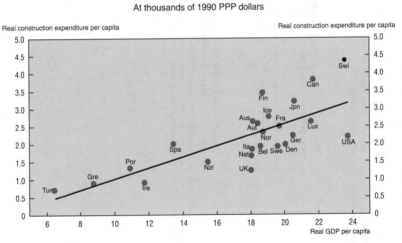

Source: OECD, *Purchasing power parities and real expenditures.*

(continued on next page)

(continued)

But it is clear that the extent to which construction expenditure in Switzerland exceeds that in other OECD countries cannot be explained entirely by high income levels. Among other factors explaining this phenomenon are climate and topography. Switzerland has cold winters, necessitating greater expenditure for building insulation and heating systems. As can be seen in Diagram 24, countries with harsh winters tend to spend more on construction than would be predicted on the basis of their levels of GDP per head. With respect to topography, Switzerland's mountainous terrain clearly has costly implications (such as many tunnels) for public works.

Another factor contributing to high real construction expenditure is likely to be Switzerland's low real mortgage interest rates, which encourage greater investment in housing. Mortgage interest rates in Switzerland are well below those in other European countries (Table 17). Over 1990-92, real rates averaged 1.6 per cent, less than half the rates in neighbouring countries. These low rates essentially reflect the generally low level of real interest rates in Switzerland – the margin between mortgage interest rates and government bond rates is similar to that in many other European countries.

Table 17. **Mortgage interest rates**

Percentage

	Average real rate			Average of mortgage rate – government bond yield		
	1980-84	1985-89	1990-92	1980-84	1985-89	1990-92
Switzerland	1.0	3.3	1.6	0.6	1.0	0.8
Austria	6.3	7.7	4.0	2.7	2.7	1.0
Belgium	6.8	6.8	5.0	1.5	0.6	1.3
Denmark	8.8	7.5	n.a.	0.8	1.5	n.a.
France	n.a.	6.2	3.9	n.a.	0.5	0.2
Germany	4.1	5.7	3.9	n.a.	0.7	0.8
Netherlands	5.6	6.9	3.9	1.1	1.0	0.5
United Kingdom	3.1	7.0	3.9	–0.1	2.1	1.5

Source: OECD, *Financial Statistics Monthly.* For Austria: Czerny, M. *et al.,* ''Zur Neugestaltung der Wohnungspolitik in Österreich'', WIFO, Wien, 1990.

Finally, the demanding quality standards and norms discussed in this chapter also appear to contribute to the high levels of real construction expenditure in Switzerland.

initiatives designed to enhance competitive pressures in construction and related sectors.

Reform of local authority regulations which restrict competition is also being considered. In the case of the ancillary industries, a reform which will be particularly important is the mutual recognition of water connection permits. This will enable firms to install bathroom or kitchen fittings in local authority areas outside their own without having to purchase additional permits. The result should be greater competition in these industries and their reorganisation; artisanal methods of production should give way to greater specialisation, with firms developing which undertake the complete installation of bathrooms or kitchens, as occurs in other countries.

Studies are also underway to identify regulations and norms which add unnecessarily to construction costs. In this respect, the federal government is reviewing norms and standards for its construction projects (buildings and national roads) and for subsidised housing with a view to eliminating specification features which are not judged to be worth what they cost; lower levels of government, which account for around 80 per cent of government construction expenditure, are not yet engaged in the same process. Construction norms should also become less costly through harmonisation with the European Union (EU). Professional and technical associations in the construction industry, and in particular the SIA, which is responsible for construction norms, are participating in the European Normalisation Committee which is preparing the EU directive on construction materials. These norms will replace those presently in place and facilitate trade in both construction materials and in construction services (such as those of architects, engineers and construction companies).

The federal government has also identified a number of other ways in which the costs of construction regulation could be reduced. One of the main reforms which would reduce such costs is to harmonise construction rules across the country. This would not only reduce compliance costs for those wishing to supply construction and related services – especially architectural and engineering services – to all cantons, but would also eliminate inconsistencies between different sets of rules (such as insulation and fire safety rules). Another way to cut regulatory costs would be to reduce delays in obtaining the necessary authorisations for a project by having closer co-operation between project planners and the authorities and by simplifying administrative procedures.

The proposed reform of competition law (another aspect of the revitalisation package) would also reduce construction costs (and indeed, prices in many other sectors). This reform would prohibit agreements to share areas of distribution and/or to control the amount of production or prices. The burden of proof required for the Cartels Commission to rule a cartel illegal would be reduced by replacing the present requirement to prove that harm results from a cartel agreement with a presumption of harm. These reforms would bring Swiss competition law more closely in line with that in other OECD countries and would ban practices which presently exist in Switzerland but are illegal in most other OECD countries.

Reform of the Lex Friedrich – the law which restricts foreign ownership of real estate and, consequently, presents a barrier to foreign competition in the construction sector – has also been proposed. This reform would remove the barrier to foreign construction companies in the area of social housing – authorisation would be given to foreign companies to buy land to develop social housing or to buy new or old social housing properties; but the barrier would remain for other building projects.[71]

Procurement policies at the federal and cantonal levels of government are also being reformed. These reforms, which flow from the recent GATT agreement, prohibit discrimination (on a reciprocal basis) against foreign competitors in the awarding of public contracts. The agreement is not, however, binding on local government, which accounts for around 48 per cent of government construction expenditure. The federal government is considering how local government can be encouraged to comply with the GATT agreement.

Land development planning

One of the key principles of the law on land development planning (Loi sur l'aménagement du territoire or LAT) – in force since 1980 – is to maintain strict separation between three designated land uses: protected zones (protection of nature, historical sites, etc.), agricultural zones, and zones where construction is allowed.[72] A striking feature of Swiss zoning law is its stark differentiation of agricultural and urban zones. This goes well beyond the rural-urban designation observed in many other countries: in principle, it prohibits the construction in agricultural zones of any structure not related to traditional agricultural use of land.[73]

Lands zoned for construction consist of two parts: land which is already used for building purposes and "reserve" lands which are scheduled to be developed for construction in the coming fifteen years. About 18 per cent of the land which could potentially be built on[74] is currently zoned for construction. Of this, 30 to 70 per cent (depending on the region) is held in reserve for future construction needs. The supply of building land is further restricted by landowners' tendency to leave land that has been zoned for construction idle. The motives behind this are numerous: the expectation of a capital gain (especially if the owner suspects the land will soon be provided with improved public services) or the desire to avoid taxes.[75] The lack of key infrastructure facilities (such as sewerage, electricity supply and roads, which are in principle provided by the local governments) is another factor limiting the supply of building land. The fact that reserve lands are not provided with public services reflects local sentiments, either that further residential construction is not needed or that it is not desirable.

Switzerland is already subjecting its land use policies to close scrutiny. This will give rise eventually to some alteration in the definitions in the broad categories of land use: protected, agricultural and urban. However, housing availability could be much improved without major changes to the zoning categories. Much could be done to encourage a more judicious use of already urbanised lands. Here the focus of initiatives will probably be on tax policy, transportation and user charging for public services (Flückiger, 1989). The Federal Council has proposed to reform the law on land development planning to permit private development of infrastructure and has submitted this project for consultation with interested parties. Similarly, there is considerable scope for more intensive construction and for renovation of old buildings. The revision of the LAT currently under way in the context of "Swisslex" should harmonise and accelerate the diverse authorisation procedures adopted by local governments and simplify the rules concerning environmental impact studies, thereby making it easier to build in areas already zoned for construction.

Housing

The features just discussed – high absolute construction prices and high prices for land on which it is possible to build – may have contributed to what is perceived in Switzerland to be a shortage of residential units. Indeed, the vacancy

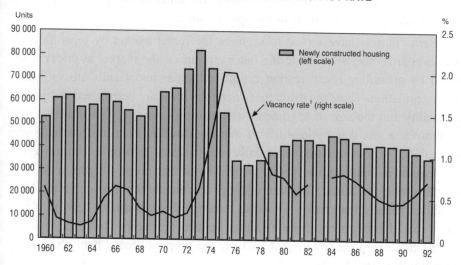

Diagram 24. **NEW HOUSING AND THE VACANCY RATE**

Units / %

Newly constructed housing
(left scale)

Vacancy rate[1] (right scale)

1. Break in series in 1983.

Source: Office fédéral de la statistique, *Statistical Yearbook of Switzerland;* OECD estimates.

rate – at well under 1 per cent in 1992 – appears to be unusually low[76] (Diagram 24). Regulations protecting tenants may have contributed to this situation, while other aspects of housing policy (including construction and ownership subsidies and relaxation of the regulations on the use of equity in occupational pension plans) have attempted to boost residential construction and the rate of home ownership. This section reviews these two, countervailing sets of policy.

Protection of tenants

The rental market has been subject to pervasive intervention for much of this century. Strict controls on rents were instituted in 1936, but were partially liberalised in 1954. In 1962, state monitoring of rents was instituted, but was later progressively liberalised over an 18-month period, during which rents increased rapidly. The current regulation – implemented in order to stem these increases – came into effect in June 1972 and was amended and incorporated in the ordinary civil law in 1989. According to the current legislation, rent increases are not considered "abusive" if they are justified by an increase in costs (mortgage rates, for example) or by additional services (renovation), if they maintain the purchasing power of the investment (compensation for inflation) or if they are in line with the rent levels prevailing in the specific area.

Rent controls have served to segment the rental market by separating old dwellings from the new. While the latter are put on the market at prices determined by prevailing rental market conditions, older rental units are subject to heavy regulation. Thus, the differences between rents are determined not just by the quality and the size of apartments, but also by their age. This situation may account for a less-than-optimal use of existing dwellings inasmuch as it lowers the mobility of tenants. It is particularly unfavourable to people who have jobs that require mobility and to young people (who tend to pay higher rents than other households). Since allocation of older apartments is not made on the basis of market rents, other criteria – such as tenants' characteristics – tend to play a major role. Furthermore, these measures reduce the returns to rental housing construction over time and ultimately damp the supply of rental housing, thereby contributing to its scarcity.

By defining specific guidelines for rent determination, current regulatory practices appear to go beyond what is required to support effective contracting in the rental sector.[77] A federal commission has been charged with studying the liberalisation of the rental market. Without taking a position one way or another, the Commission clarified the advantages and disadvantages of such a move and proposed measures that would need to accompany liberalisation. According to a study by Schips and Müller (1993), a reasonable estimate of the increase in average rents due to a lifting of rent controls is roughly SF 5 billion. In order to buffer against the shock of such a wealth transfer from tenants to owners, the Commission proposes that, if enacted, liberalisation be spread out over ten years and that compensation be paid to economically disadvantaged tenants.[78]

Encouraging home ownership and the construction of new housing

Switzerland is essentially a country of tenants. It has the lowest rate of home ownership among a group of fourteen OECD countries (Diagram 25). Only 31.3 per cent of dwellings were owner-occupied in 1990. This rate was 37 per cent in 1950, but fell to 28.1 per cent in 1970 as a result of the strong immigration waves of the fifties and sixties.[79]

A number of steps have been taken to increase the rate of owner-occupancy. Policies in the area of occupational pensions funds ("prévoyance profession-

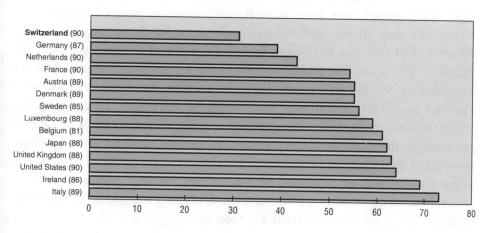

Diagram 25. **SHARE OF OWNER-OCCUPIED HOUSING IN SELECTED COUNTRIES**[1]

1. Date in brackets is the census year.
Source: Office fédéral de la statistique, *Statistical Yearbook of Switzerland 1994;* United Nations, *Housing in the world,* New York, 1993.

nelle'') have been altered so as to encourage home ownership. This amendment is scheduled to take effect in January 1995. The change allows people covered by occupational pensions to use part of their accumulated equity in the fund to acquire an owner-occupied dwelling, to pay down existing mortgage debt or to purchase shares in a housing co-operative. Covered employees will be able to use all of their accumulated pension equity if they are under 50 years old. People over 50 may obtain the value of their accumulated equity at the age of 50 or half of their accumulated equity at the time they make the request.

This initiative's prospects for encouraging home ownership and construction are difficult to quantify. The Federal Council's message presenting the project anticipates a short-term boost in demand for residential construction of 10 to 20 per cent, but of only 3 to 5 per cent in the long run. The allocation of new acquisitions between existing structures and new constructions is also highly uncertain. The ability of younger pension contributors to purchase a home will not be much affected since their equity stake would tend to be quite small.

A federal programme initiated in 1974 encourages new housing construction and home ownership.[80] The programme authorises loan guarantees and interest subsidies for developing and improving sites, loan guarantees for real estate developers and co-operatives and loans made under preferential conditions for more disadvantaged borrowers. In most years, assistance under the programme affects less than 10 per cent of total building output. Since the law became effective, 110 000 dwellings have been built, acquired or renovated with the benefit of federal aid. The grants provided by the federal government for housing amounted to SF 140 million in 1992. In addition, federal guarantees were extended on mortgages and other loans worth SF 4.3 billion. To complete this picture of housing assistance, one must add a variety of outlays made by cantons and municipalities and the amounts earmarked for housing under general welfare spending. Taken together, the payments made under all programmes by all levels of government add up to around SF 500 million per year, compared with an annual housing construction volume of some SF 17 billion per year. The amounts of money involved, then, are relatively modest.

A recent report[81] analysing the impact of the 1974 law concludes that it has contributed to the achievement of its stated objectives. The report notes, neverthe-less, that 35 to 50 per cent of households receiving such assistance would have bought a dwelling even in the absence of the programme. It also notes the contradiction that may exist between the law's objectives – increasing owner occupancy and housing construction – and rent controls, which enhance the attractiveness of renting and lower the return on rental housing construction.

Assessment

This examination of the policy environment surrounding housing, construc-tion and land use points – as is the case for many other countries – to the difficulty of finding an appropriate policy mix when so many, often conflicting goals are being pursued. Zoning regulations that control development have largely succeeded in preserving the natural beauty of much of the Swiss country-side, but have added to housing costs. Attempts to protect tenants' interests have progressively shifted incentives away from home ownership and have discour-aged new housing development. Regulations addressing legitimate needs for product and service standards, combined with a rather tolerant competition pol-icy, have been used by firms in construction and related industries in support of anti-competitive practices.

In looking at high housing, construction and land prices, it is by no means easy to separate the policy influences from those of other factors (high incomes, topography, etc.).[82] Looked at as a whole, however, the policy framework does seem to have been an important contributor to high housing costs and to the apparent scarcity of housing. In any case, investors in housing development seem to attach considerable importance to the policy environment. Two consecutive surveys[83] – one done in 1982 and the other in 1992 – attest to this. According to the 1982 study, the scarcity of land on which is was possible to build was the main factor that restricted the construction of new dwellings. The second most important factor cited was municipal and cantonal restrictions on construction, while high construction costs came in third. The more recent report showed that financing conditions were viewed as being most important, followed closely by tenants' protection (according to the report, the effect of rent controls was to shift construction away from new dwellings and toward renovation of old dwellings). High land prices were in third place. Thus, investors' decisions do appear to be heavily influenced by variables that are either directly controlled by the government (rent control, building restrictions) or that are influenced by the government (construction costs, land prices).

Finding the right balance between conflicting objectives – and in this case the major conflict is between the need to preserve the quality of the Swiss living environment and the desire to lower housing costs – is a major challenge for government. Recent initiatives in the treatment of occupational pensions and in competition policy indicate that government wishes to lower housing costs and to encourage owner-occupancy. There would seem to be ample scope for promoting these objectives without detracting from the beauty of the Swiss landscape and without embarking on new programmes or extending old subsidies. Increasing competitive pressures in construction and related sectors through enhanced enforcement of competition policy is the most obvious candidate. Tax policy, infrastructure management and user charges for public services could encourage more intensive use of existing urban zones. Tenant protection in its current form seems to go well beyond the contractual guarantees that are necessary to promote a well functioning rental market. Finally, zoning – especially of agricultural land – and the desirability of more extensive residential use of non-urban zones need to be rethought and indeed, are the subject of an ongoing discussion.[84]

V. Conclusions

After about two and a half years of sluggish activity the Swiss economy bottomed out during the summer of 1993, finishing the longest but – in terms of the drop in output – not the deepest recession since the war. The economic upswing in the second half of 1993 was broadly based, with machinery and equipment investment being particularly buoyant. For 1993 as a whole, however, real GDP fell slightly, and the current external surplus rose further, to a record high of 8 per cent of GDP. In the spring of 1994, current and forward-looking indicators suggest that the Swiss economy is keeping an upward momentum. With employment picking up and consumer confidence progressively reviving in the course of 1994, household consumption should gather strength. Machinery and equipment investment is likely to continue its recent upswing, reflecting ongoing efforts of enterprises to modernise productive capacity, as well as reduced credit costs and lower prices of imported investment goods. The fall in short-term interest rates combined with recovering demand should also induce a progressive build-up of inventories. But subdued household incomes and the high stock of unused office space will continue to act as a brake on total construction investment. Exports are likely to strengthen, reflecting vigorous growth of export markets, while import demand too should recover. With the real foreign balance deteriorating, but the terms of trade improving further and net investment income remaining buoyant, the current external surplus may decline only slightly, to $7^{1}/_{4}$ per of GDP in 1994 and to $6^{3}/_{4}$ per cent in 1995.

In spite of the shallowness of the recent recession, employment fell sharply and unemployment surged to record highs, being at the end of 1993 about ten times its extremely low level of 1990. This brought to the fore a social problem relatively unknown hitherto, namely that of high long-term unemployment. The probability of the long-term unemployed finding a job declines progressively and they risk dropping out of the labour market and the unemployment benefit system altogether. Youth unemployment, however, still remains a minor problem compared with most other OECD countries. Registered unemployment may stabilise in 1994 as the projected average contraction of employment is expected to be offset by reduced labour supply, in particular of seasonal and frontier workers. The labour market should show clearer signs of improvement in 1995, when higher capacity utilisation calls for growing labour input.

The widening gap between actual and potential output brought inflation down, but since assistance from exchange rate appreciation came later this time than in earlier episodes of macroeconomic stabilisation, the process of disinflation took an unusually long time. Only in the spring of 1994, more than five and a half years after monetary policy changed course, did the twelve-month rate of consumer price inflation come down to 1 per cent, the upper limit of what the Swiss National Bank deems tolerable in the medium term. In June 1994, the 12-month headline inflation rate was 0.5 per cent. Given the recent exchange rate appreciation and the existing slack in the economy, consumer price inflation should stay low and average about 1 per cent for 1994. But the replacement of the present turnover tax on goods by a general value-added tax at the beginning of 1995 could raise recorded CPI inflation temporarily to 2½ per cent in 1995.

The general government budget deficit reached an unprecedented 4.5 per cent of GDP in 1993. About half of the total deficit is estimated to be of a cyclical nature and should disappear once the economy approaches potential output. Owing to this cyclical effect and discretionary measures that have been taken to bring the structural part of the deficit under better control, the general government deficit may decline by ¾ per cent of GDP during the two years to 1995. This represents a shift to a slightly restrictive stance of fiscal policy.

As the current setting of Swiss fiscal policy fails to achieve the government's medium-term goal of a balanced budget, further consolidation efforts will be required to meet this objective. Although current budget plans should be sufficient to stabilise the general government debt-to-GDP ratio, the OECD estimates that this ratio would only stabilise at around 55 per cent – a ratio which the Swiss government considers to be too high. In any case, such calculations are subject to uncertainty. For example, they are based on the assumption that the rate of unemployment will fall to 2½ per cent when economic activity returns to normal levels. To the extent that the "true" non-cyclical rate of unemployment is higher, the structural part of the budget deficit is underestimated, which would mean that even greater efforts to consolidate the budget would be required. In view of such risks the Finance Department's plan to establish a new expenditure savings programme, which caps the expansion of federal expenditures to the rate of nominal GDP growth in the coming four years, is appropriate.

Apart from raising additional federal revenues, the replacement of the antiquated turnover tax on goods – which fails to tax services and energy – by a modern value-added tax is a principal step towards a less distortive tax system. The present turnover tax is levied not only on consumer goods but also on investment goods and intermediate inputs each time a market transaction takes place, a feature usually referred to as the hidden tax (*"taxe occulte"*). The hidden tax can be presumed to have had a harmful effect on investment and on international competitiveness in both export and import markets. The fact that the turnover tax on investment and intermediate inputs earns about one half of the total revenue from this source suggests that the magnitude of this effect is not negligible.

Given the current speed of the economic recovery, scope for further monetary easing appears limited. Although there still appears to be substantial slack in the economy, and therefore no imminent danger of renewed inflationary pressures, the lag between changes in monetary policy and their effects has to be taken into account. Inflation is very low now, but it will increase temporarily in 1995 due to the introduction of value-added tax. Some further upward pressure on prices may emerge as the economic upswing gains speed. The monetary base has picked up and the broader aggregate M1 grew strongly in the recent past. A cautious attitude of the SNB is thus appropriate to lock in the achieved price stability. OECD projections are based on the assumption that the SNB will accept some further decline in short-term interest rates along with the assumed decline in German interest rates.

The question of the appropriate monetary policy stance in the near term is inseparably linked with the issue of the adequate intermediate target of monetary policy. This will be particularly important at the end of 1994, when the Swiss National Bank (SNB) will have to decide on what should guide its policy in 1995 and beyond. The question is difficult because, as in other OECD countries, legal and technological change in financial markets have raised doubts about the stability of relationships between indicators of monetary conditions, such as the

SNB's seasonally-adjusted monetary base, and nominal income or inflation. Although Switzerland may be less affected by this phenomenon than other OECD countries, it would be helpful for further empirical analysis if broader monetary aggregates, especially M1, could soon be redefined in a manner which would overcome their well-known shortcomings, thereby making them less distorted indicators of monetary conditions. Beyond these technical improvements, the SNB should continue not to rely exclusively on the signals from the monetary base.

Questions can also be raised as to whether it would be wise to aim at keeping consumer price inflation durably within the rather narrow 0 to 1 per cent range. In spite of the recession, the GDP deflator – a useful indicator of "underlying" or "core" inflation – remained stuck at around $2\frac{1}{2}$ per cent during 1993. To a large extent this reflects the stickiness of Swiss service prices, which is in part due to the fact that measured productivity growth in the services sector tends to be lower than that in goods producing industries. Moreover, the SNB's task is complicated by the well-known fact that the consumer price index (CPI) tends to overstate true price inflation to the extent that the index fails to capture certain quality improvements of goods and services as well as the emergence of new products and services. If the SNB is to pursue rigorously the stated inflation goal, support from structural policies to bring greater downward flexibility to service prices would be helpful.

A genuine source of service price stickiness is that many services are protected from foreign competition. Hence, it appears that a promising way to enhance the downward flexibility of prices is to expose non-tradables or protected goods and services to more intense domestic and foreign competition. This would not only help to reduce existing "monopoly rents" but also spur productivity. The government's first revitalisation package of reforms goes a long way in this direction. Once fully implemented, it would increase competitive pressures in Switzerland and align commercial laws and regulations more closely with those in the European Union. A particularly important aspect of this package is a complete revision of the legislation against anti-competitive practices. The proposed legislation takes a tougher line against cartels and certain abuses of dominant positions, especially by introducing harm presumption clauses for cartels directly or indirectly setting prices, restricting the volume of goods or services (for purchase or supply) or dividing up the market on a territorial basis. New laws are also being proposed, aimed at reducing technical barriers to international trade and at limiting the scope for local government and municipalities to erect barriers to trade through protectionist regulations. In view of the importance of these measures for improvements in productivity and living standards, it is vital that they be put into effect as quickly as possible.

The Federal Council has announced a second wave of microeconomic reforms. These reforms would relax the Post Office's monopoly in telecommunications and postal services, strengthen the long-term financial position of the old-age pension fund, introduce maternity assurance and reduce agricultural export subsidies (in line with the GATT agreement) as well as corporate income taxes. While the planned reforms would represent some progress towards creating an environment more conducive to higher productivity, an even more ambitious programme in many of these areas would be desirable on economic grounds (for example, greater liberalisation of telecommunications and agricultural markets).

A series of measures – notably an increase in unemployment insurance contribution rates – has been taken to stem the losses being incurred by the unemployment insurance fund due to the recent unprecedented levels of unemployment. Further measures are under parliamentary debate, including an additional increase in contribution rates and a tripling of the ceiling on gross salaries. The definition of a reasonable job offer has been widened, in order to deal with the problem of "moral hazard". The law on sickness insurance has also been revised. The changes introduced make coverage mandatory and pave the way for new forms of insurance and health care delivery. This should result in greater competition between providers of health care. As from 1995 the law governing employer pension schemes will be changed so as to eliminate the losses formerly incurred by employees transferring funds to another scheme. This measure should enhance labour market mobility.

Construction expenditure in Switzerland represents one of the highest proportions of GDP amongst OECD countries. In part, this reflects Switzerland's high standard of living – in general, the richer a country, the larger the proportion of income spent on construction. But the extent of the difference between the Swiss construction ratio and those of other OECD countries is such that other factors must also be at work. While international comparisons show that Swiss construction costs are relatively high, they are no more so than Swiss prices in general – hence, high costs cannot explain the high construction to GDP ratio.

Rather, demanding specifications for buildings in terms of features and quality would appear to be one of the major explanatory factors. Indeed, a study which compared construction costs for similar apartment buildings in Switzerland and Germany found that half of the difference in price could be accounted for by the higher specifications for equipment and construction quality in the Swiss building. Also, many of the additional specification requirements in Switzerland were found to be superfluous to meeting the demands of the project as specified by the client. This difference between the real and imposed needs of the client provides scope to reduce housing costs, especially for social housing. As part of the additional requirements reflect regulations, there is a case for reviewing them.

Construction costs could also be reduced by increasing competitive pressures in the sector. In this respect, harmonisation of norms and standards in the kitchen and bathroom fittings industries with those of the EC should be particularly helpful. Moreover, the envisaged new law against cartels should permit the dissolution of other cartels in the building materials industries. There would also appear to be considerable scope to reduce costs for public works undertaken for local governments and municipalities by having more open and competitive tendering arrangements.

Like many other countries, Switzerland also faces a host of issues relating to land use and housing. Within a context of rigid land use regulations, the supply of land which can be built on has been reduced by the limited development of available sites, even in urban zones. This reflects, in part, further private decisions to leave land idle, which may in turn be related to the high construction costs noted above, to tax policy and to pervasive rent controls. It also reflects the reluctance of local governments to extend public services to undeveloped urban zones, either because they view it as excessively costly relative to the expected improvement in their tax base or because they wish to slow urban development. In any case, high land prices have helped lift housing prices, and this has contributed to the low proportion of owner-occupiers in Switzerland.

Intervention in the rental market – involving rent controls on large parts of the housing stock – also appear to have damped the supply of residential units. Other policies affecting housing – financial aids for residential construction and home ownership and the more recent decision to relax rules for occupational pension funds in order to allow parts of the accumulated equity to be used for purchase of a home – indicate that the government desires to lift housing supply and to encourage home ownership. In attempting to do so, the government should seek to place any new initiatives within a coherent overall mix of policies. Priority should be given to eliminating structural features which needlessly lift housing costs and restrict supply. In this respect, policies to increase competitive pressures in construction and related industries and to liberalise rent controls would seem to be natural first steps.

To sum up, the economic upswing currently under way and the low rate of inflation now achieved will lay the basis for reducing labour market imbalances and for trimming government budget deficits. But the favourable outlook should not give rise to complacency. Challenging tasks are ahead. Targeting the monetary base by the SNB needs to be complemented by careful monitoring of a broad range of indicators to detect as early as possible any changes in the indicative properties of the monetary base. Costs of achieving the ambitious inflation objectives will have to be lowered by reducing structural impediments to price flexibility. Stepped-up efforts in structural reforms, as represented by the revitalisation and the Swisslex projects, are necessary if the Swiss economy is to benefit fully from the growing process of international integration. Pursuit of these complementary policies gives the best hope for attaining a sustainable increase in the standard of living.

Notes

1. Chapter II of last year's OECD *Survey of Switzerland* contains a detailed analysis of factors heralding economic downturns and upswings. It concluded that if the mechanisms identified were stable then the following upswing should take place in the autumn of 1993.

2. The Konjunkturforschungsstelle (KOF) in Zürich expects this first official estimate of the National Accounts to be revised upward later on when more detailed information is available on those construction projects which do not require official authorisation.

3. An official disaggregation of construction investment is not available yet. Figures used here are KOF estimates, which suggest that public construction volumes grew by 1¾ per cent in 1993.

4. The official estimate of the subsidised investment volume assumes that all of it represents new projects, entirely induced by the government programme, which appears rather unrealistic.

5. Earlier OECD Secretariat estimates suggest a relatively high interest elasticity of Swiss business investment, which is in accordance with other research. Cf. the 1988/89 OECD *Economic Survey of Switzerland,* Chapter II, and Annex I, "A model of the supply side of the Swiss economy".

6. Swiss authorities generally assume – explicitly or implicitly – potential output growth of 2 per cent, which is equal to the actual long-term average rate of growth.

7. In 1975, household incomes suffered from an exceptionally steep fall in employment. In 1982, real disposable personal incomes grew by a solid 1¾ per cent, but the saving ratio increased by more than 1½ percentage points.

8. *Cf.* Cornioley, C. (1994), "La situation des jeunes au chômage", *La Vie économique,* April.

9. A federal decree authorises an increase of rents by 2 to 3 per cent for each quarter of a percentage point increase in the mortgage rate, depending on the actual level of the mortgage rate. With a weight of 22 per cent in the consumer price index (CPI), the impact of rents on general consumer price inflation is substantial. The discontinuous effect of housing rent changes on the CPI stems from their being recorded every three months only (February, May, August and November).

10. As from May 1993, the wholesale price index has been replaced by the total supply price index, which is the weighted sum of producer price index and import price index. The new index has been linked with the old wholesale price index.

11. The comparatively low intensity of competition and its impact on price persistence were discussed in the 1991/92 OECD *Economic Survey of Switzerland,* Part III.

12. If the supply price index, which rose by a mere 0.2 per cent in 1993, were the relevant index for entrepreneurs, the so derived real wage rate would have risen by about $2^1/_2$ per cent.

13. About 40 per cent of the collective wage agreements contain inflation compensation clauses. In general, these clauses specify an adjustment of contractual wages to the twelve-monthly inflation of the preceding October, but none of them stipulates fully automatic indexation.

14. Tobin's q equals the market value of shares and business bonds divided by the replacement value of the capital stock. It may also be expressed as the ratio of the rate of return on capital to the cost of capital. Cf. the 1992/93 OECD *Survey of Switzerland,* Chapter II.

15. The seasonally-adjusted monetary base consists of notes in circulation and sight deposits held with the National Bank. In addition to its seasonal adjustment, the series is corrected for the biennial peak in note circulation at the end of even years, when property and income taxes are assessed, because of evidence that taxpayers try to reduce their tax base by converting parts of their financial assets into currency.

16. The precise base period of the current targeting exercise was made public only in December 1992, two years after the change in its general approach had been announced by the National Bank. Cf. "La politique monétaire suisse en 1993", *Monnaie et conjoncture,* Bulletin trimestriel de la Banque nationale suisse, December 1992.

17. For more details see the monetary policy sections of the 1989/90 and 1990/91 OECD *Economic Surveys of Switzerland.*

18. *Cf.* "La politique monétaire suisse en 1994", *Monnaie et conjoncture,* Bulletin trimestriel de la Banque nationale suisse, December 1993.

19. Indeed, attaining the SNB's monetary target at the end of 1994 would require an acceleration of the growth of the SAMB to a twelve-monthly rate of about $4^1/_2$ per cent in the fourth quarter of 1994. At first sight, this may appear not unlikely, given that the SAMB grew at an annual rate of about 4 per cent during the first five months of 1994. However, the growth of the demand for bank notes is expected to slow down as interest rates on savings deposits have stopped falling.

20. For a discussion of potential alternatives to base money targeting see, for example, the OECD *Economic Survey of Switzerland 1991/92,* Part II.

21. *Cf.* Banque nationale suisse, *86ᵉ rapport de gestion, 1994,* p. 10.

22. Because the highly-liquid interest-bearing salary accounts *("comptes salaires")* were not recorded by commercial banks in a uniform way, they were excluded from M1 and M2, but included in M3 by the revision of Swiss monetary statistics in 1985. However, their widespread use for payments makes an M1 which does not include them an incomplete indicator of money held for transaction purposes. At present, work is being done by the National Bank to overcome these problems.

23. See Banque nationale suisse, *Bulletin mensuel,* April 1994, p. 6. Revised figures for broad monetary aggregates were for the first time published in that issue of the Bulletin.

24. As measured by an index of trade-weighted relative consumer prices in common currency.

25. For a brief summary see Part II of the 1990/91 OECD *Economic Survey of Switzerland.*

26. Applying ordinary least squares regression analysis, an equation of the following specification has been estimated on quarterly data from the first quarter of 1974 to the fourth quarter of 1993 (t-values are in brackets):

$$\text{IRL-IRL}(-1) = 0.124 + 0.246 \text{ (IRL.GER-IRL.GER}(-1)) + 0.039 \text{ (PCP-PCP.GER)}$$

(2.19)   (4.30)   (2.75)

$$-3.107 \text{ (CB/GDP)} + 0.163 \text{ (IRS-IRS}(-1)) + 0.009 \text{ (DGDPV-DGDPV.GER)}$$

(–2.58)   (5.57)   (2.69)

$$R^2 = 0.71 \qquad \text{D.W.} = 1.99 \qquad \text{S.E.E.} = 0.19$$

IRL is the bond rate, IRS the Zürich three-month deposit rate, PCP the percentage change in the consumer price deflator, CB the current external balance, GDP the nominal gross domestic product and DGDPV the growth rate of real GDP. Variables without suffix refer to Switzerland, those with the tag ".GER" refer to the corresponding German variable. The equation seeks to explain the change in the Confederation bond rate by the change in the German long-term bond rate, the Swiss-German inflation differential, the scaled current external balance, the change in Swiss short-term interest rate and the Swiss-German growth differential.

27. See the discussion in Aeberhardt, W., and M. Zumstein, *Zinsinsel Schweiz,* Bundesamt für Konjunkturfragen, Studie Nr. 13, Bern 1990. The authors express doubts as to whether Swiss interest rates can be persistently lower than abroad p. 65).

28. This includes old-age insurance (AVS), unemployment insurance (AC), disability insurance (AI), loss-of-earnings insurance (APG) and accident insurance (CNA).

29. Among the OECD countries for which data are available only the gross debt/GDP ratio of Australia – at 34.2 per cent – was below that of Switzerland in 1993. The OECD average amounted to 66 per cent in 1993. However, gross debt figures give a misleading impression of public indebtedness for countries where the public sector holds substantial amounts of financial assets, for example Japan and the United States. Unfortunately, net general government debt series are not available for Switzerland. But general government financial assets are unlikely to be substantial relative to GDP.

30. A medium-term debt scenario is sketched out at the end of this section.

31. The federal direct tax is calculated on the basis of two years' average income, with 50 per cent being levied, after a one-year lag, in each of the two subsequent years. Since the first year of the collection period is always an even year, the system results in strong growth of tax revenues in even years and a tendency to stabilisation in odd years, whatever the phase of the business cycle. For example, the revenues from the federal direct tax in 1993 were the second annual payment of the two-yearly collection period 1992/93, which refers to incomes that accrued in the cyclically strong years 1989 and 1990. A similar procedure applies to income tax levied by most cantons and communes, with a somewhat shorter lag. Although the cyclical fluctuation of the Swiss economy could be dampened if a more timely assessment and collection of direct taxes on all incomes were introduced, this proposal found no majority in the Parliament.

32. The above-mentioned lags between the accrual of incomes and their taxation, which differ between the Confederation and cantons as well as between cantons, complicate the breakdown of actual budget balances into cyclical and structural components for Switzerland. The

figures used in this section have been provided by the "Office fédéral des questions conjoncturelles" and are based on the same methodology as that of the OECD Secretariat, adjusted, however, to the idiosyncrasies of the Swiss tax system. For details cf. Ammann, Y., "Le budget de plein emploi", *Cahiers de conjoncture*, No. 2, 1988.

33.   *Cf.* Table 18, "Indicators of the 'natural rate' of unemployment" of last year's OECD *Economic Survey of Switzerland.*

34.   Taxes on investment contribute on average about half of total revenues from (the present) turnover tax on goods, with roughly equal shares of construction and machinery and equipment investment. Since the turnover tax exempts services (roughly one-half of household consumption) and energy, the share of private consumption in total turnover tax revenues amounts to some 40 per cent only.

35.   The federal deficit for 1993 shown in the Table "Central government budget" is more than SF 1 billion below the deficit given in the Table "Government accounts" above. This is so because the former is based on the definition of the Confederation's financial accounting system which neutralises the Confederation's interest payments and contributions to the Federal Insurance Fund *("Caisse fédérale d'assurance")* by commensurate revenues. The federal government figures of the Table "Government accounts", however, use the definition of the "Statistique financière révisée", which make them comparable with the cantons' and communes' accounting systems and allow their aggregation to general government finances.

36.   At first sight, the closing gap between federal revenues and expenditures as sketched out here may appear in diametrical contrast to the picture given in the *"Message concernant le budget 1994"* of the Federal Council, which signals changes of expenditures by +8.9 per cent and of revenues by –1.3 per cent. The difference between the figures rests in the customary practice of the *"Message"* to compare budget projections with the previous year's *initial* budget.

37.   Federal direct tax revenues in 1994 – the first year of a biennial collection cycle – are based on incomes accrued in 1991 and 1992, when real output stagnated, but disposable incomes were blown up by high inflation.

38.   The government established also an alternative scenario which foresees weaker real growth, but at the current juncture, the baseline case appears more realistic.

39.   The federal government's first fiscal consolidation package was approved by the Parliament in October 1992 and consisted of specific tax increases, notably a rise in the import duty on petrol by SF 0.20 per litre, and cuts in expenditures, in particular a linear cut by 10 per cent of a variety of transfer payments. The latter measure is, however, targeted to expire at the end of 1995. The annual budgetary relief from the package amounts to about SF 4 billion (SF 2 billion each on the expenditure and revenue side). As part of the initial draft consolidation package the government had also proposed to amend the Constitution to the effect that an absolute majority of the members of Parliament were required for decisions to raise expenditures above government proposals ("freins aux dépenses"). This is still under parliamentary discussion. For more details see the *OECD Economic Survey of Switzerland 1991/1992,* Chapter II.

40.   Official budget projections are available for the federal government until 1997, but for lower levels of government for 1994 only. The debt scenario assumes that the ratio of the primary cyclically-adjusted budget balance to GDP of the federal government remains constant from

1996 onwards and that that of the cantons and communes stays at their 1994 levels. The scenario also adopts the assumptions of the Confederation's medium-term financial plan for real growth (2 per cent), inflation (2½ per cent) and the long-term interest rate (4½ per cent).

41. The PCAB required to stabilise the debt ratio is obtained from the dynamic government budget constraint:

$$db = PCAB + ((r - g)/(1 + g)) *b$$

where

    db is the change in the debt-to-GDP ratio,

    r   is the real interest rate,

    g   is the growth rate of real GDP,

    b   is the initial debt-to-GDP ratio.

To have a stable debt-to-GDP ratio, PCAB must equal the product of the initial debt-to-GDP ratio and the difference between the real interest rate and growth rate. If the real interest rate equals the growth rate, as in the official assumptions, the required PCAB for debt stability is zero. In the event that the real interest rate were below the growth rate, there would be no sustainability problem, regardless of the fiscal deficit; the government could issue debt without ever having to reimburse it. During the past, conditions in Switzerland came close to such a favourable scenario: during the past 35 years, the average annual Confederation bond rate exceeded the rate of growth of nominal GDP only in seven cases, all related to recessions.

42. "Issues in the current tax reform" were discussed in some detail in the 1989/90 OECD *Economic Survey of Switzerland,* Chapter IV, and were updated in the 1990/91 and 1991/92 OECD *Economic Surveys of Switzerland.*

43. The tax base is weakened further by the exemption from taxation of a variety of goods, among them food items, non-alcoholic beverages, water, medicine, books, newspapers, and certain agricultural products.

44. These reforms are unilateral. In some instances, such as the regulations on animal epidemics, the reforms will be sufficient to liberalise trade with the EC. However, in others,such as producer liability, it will also be necessary to negotiate an agreement with the EC.

45. Under the existing legislative procedure, the preliminary draft of a proposed measure is sent to the cantons, political parties and other interested groups for consultation. The government then transmits this draft, amended in the light of the consultations, to Parliament in the form of a "message". The two chambers then decide on its final content. Most changes are subject to a facultative referendum.

46. Of a total length of 125 km, including a new 57 km-long base tunnel under the Gotthard, and a 55 km-long section, of which 33 km of tunnel, through the Lotschberg. The total cost of the project will be about SF 14 billion.

47. The ceiling is presently SF 97 200 per year, which is less than twice the average gross salary.

48. The public sector owns only 2.7 per cent of dwellings (1990 housing census); the other major groups of owners of dwellings are private individuals (68.7 per cent of dwellings), co-operatives, insurance companies and pension funds (18.1 per cent of dwellings) and firms

(10.5 per cent). Government assistance for the construction of dwellings (including public housing) is somewhat higher but, nevertheless, typically involves less than 10 per cent of dwellings constructed; the major exception was in the early 1990s, when the proportion was almost 30 per cent. Such assistance varies inversely with the business cycle.

49. Office fédéral de statistiques (1994), *Les statistiques annuelles de la construction,* Berne.

50. All construction sectors, including metallic construction and other construction activities, such as landscaping.

51. These industries include those providing consulting services (such as architects, engineers and surveyors) and building materials.

52. It should be noted, however, that employment statistics show that employment in the (narrowly defined) construction sector was 9.8 per cent of total employment in the third quarter of 1991. However, this figure is probably an underestimate as it does not take into account the results of the federal businesses survey.

53. These statistics come from the OECD/Eurostat joint project on purchasing power parities (PPPs). For the construction sector, they were based on quotes (including details on types and quantities of materials used) for 23 projects (8 apartment buildings, 7 non-residential buildings and 8 civil engineering projects). These estimates should be viewed as indicating broad orders of magnitude, particularly in view of the approximations required to standardise the quotes for different norms and regulations.

54. Residential construction prices are referred to because the construction price deflator in Switzerland is based on the residential price deflator and a construction price deflator is unavailable for many countries.

55. Caution is required in interpreting construction price statistics as they are based on quotes which are known to be only for statistical purposes.

56. Office fédéral du logement (1993), *Abaisser les coûts dans la construction de logements,* Rapport de travail sur le logement 27, Berne. The exchange rate used in this study was SF 90 = DM 100.

57. German prices in 1992 ranged from 13 per cent higher than Swiss prices in the north of Germany to 30 per cent higher in the south. This difference was mainly attributable to the high costs of brickwork and wooden window frames in Germany. On the other hand, prices for equipment of a comparable standard were much higher for the Swiss building; this was especially so for wiring, plumbing, kitchens and bathrooms. To some extent, Swiss construction prices were understated in this study as they had already fallen for cyclical reasons whereas the downturn in Germany had not yet impacted on prices; after increasing at broadly similar rates from January 1990 to April 1991, Swiss (Zurich) prices subsequently fell 11 per cent relative to German prices by the autumn of 1992.

58. See Chapter III of the *1991/92 OECD Survey of Switzerland* for a discussion of competition and competition policy. Lambelet (1994) provides an explanation based on a Scandinavian type of economic model comprising a productive export sector and a protected import sector. He estimates that around 60 per cent of the difference between Swiss prices and average prices in the OECD is due to high real wages in the export sector flowing through to the rest of the economy and that the remaining 40 per cent is mainly due to agricultural protection.

Lambelet, J.-Chr. (1994), *Niveau de vie et niveau des prix en Suisse et dans les autres pays de l'OCDE*, CREA, Lausanne, April.

59. The construction industry here is narrowly defined, excluding direct inputs from other sectors such as building materials, and architectural and engineering services.

60. The lower-than-average wage rates in construction reflect workers' average skill levels in this sector. The fact that construction wages are not unusually low relative to the national average in Switzerland suggests that the use of foreign workers in this sector has not markedly reduced wage rates relative to those in other countries' construction sectors.

61. Felder, S., *et al.* (1993), "The Swiss Construction Sector", in: Zweifel, P., *Services in Switzerland*, Springer-Verlag, Berlin.

62. One of the few such examples is the French company Bouygues which bought Losinger.

63. This law (which was passed in 1983 but replaced equivalent regulations dating from 1961) prohibits the purchase of land by foreigners. It also prohibits the purchase of buildings by foreigners for pure investment purposes but, subject to authorisation, does permit the purchase of a building by a subsidiary of a foreign firm for commercial purposes. The federal government has made a proposal to reform this law (see below).

64. A flagrant example of the use of restrictive conditions was the requirement for enterprises to have already constructed a bridge in the Canton of Geneva to be able to submit an offer to construct a new bridge for this canton.

65. More recent estimates obtained using the same methodology indicate that the extra cost is a minimum of 6.3 per cent. See Felder, S. (1994), "Auswirkungen der öffentlichen Vergabepolitik auf den Wettbewerbspreis in der Bauwirtschaft", *Swiss Journal of Economics and Statistics*, June.

66. Construction regulations and laws are imposed by cantons and local governments. These rules prescribe requirements for such diverse features as the percentage of land which a building may occupy (local government), the minimum size of rooms and facilities, the ratio of windows to floor space (mainly in urban areas) and insulation qualities. Construction norms and recommendations (for example, the amount of iron reinforcing in concrete) are set by the Société Suisse des Ingénieurs et des Architectes (SIA).

67. It should be noted in this regard that investors have lowered certain quality standards in recent years in order to reduce construction costs.

68. The principal way in which bureaucratic procedures inflate land values is by imposing high costs on land development for construction. The administrative procedures for installing the necessary infrastructure – such as drains, electricity and roads – are long and complicated. The federal government is encouraging local governments – which regulate access to infrastructure services – to shorten and simplify them.

69. The secretariat had in 1993 six scientific investigating staff and two junior investigating staff.

70. This cartel is only likely to be finally disbanded when the federal government imposes technical standards in line with EC norms.

71. This reform would also end the need for foreign firms to obtain authorisation to buy real estate for business purposes.

72. According to the LAT, scenery must be preserved, notably by setting aside a sufficient amount of good quality land for agriculture, by ensuring that buildings and facilities are well integrated into the scenery, by facilitating the access to lake sides and streams, and by conserving natural sites, forests and hiking zones. To attain these goals, cantons and communes elaborate detailed plans and guidelines under the surveillance of the Confederation.

73. In a context of lower agricultural supports, this obviously restricts the ability of farmers to engage in other income generating activities such as "agro-tourism" and the running of small businesses.

74. Total land surface minus rivers, very mountainous terrain, wetlands, etc.

75. Taxes on real property vary from one canton to another. Generally, though, capital gains taxes increase substantially if the property is held for shorter periods.

76. This may reflect factors other than a scarcity of rental units. Possible contributors would include a low average propensity to move and efficient home finding services.

77. It is worth noting nevertheless, that rent controls in Switzerland – which were strengthened in 1990 – are still not as severe as in some countries and, accordingly, have not had such a deleterious effect on supply. The changes in rental regulation of June 1990 allow rents to be changed as follows:
    – Rents may be increased by 40 per cent of the rate of inflation in order to maintain the purchasing power of the owner's equity investment.
    – An increase in mortgage rates may be reflected in rents. Specifically, an increase of 0.25 point translates into an increase in rental rates of 2 per cent, or of 2.5 per cent, or of 3.0 per cent depending on whether the mortgage rate is higher than 6 per cent, between 6 and 5 per cent, or less than 5 per cent.
    – The possibility to contest an increase in rents is extended to a new tenant in the case where the tenants change.

78. This compensation would be progressively phased out over the ten year implementation period and would be financed by a temporary tax on owners of rental units.

79. This low rate of home ownership obtains even with a relatively advantageous tax treatment (complete mortgage interest deduction and a conservative appraisal method for tax purposes). Several factors have been used to explain this situation. First, it only became possible to divide buildings into multiple dwellings in 1965. Second, for a large number of tenants, rents are lower than the cost of financing. Third, the high cost of housing exceeds the financial capacity of many households.

80. Tax treatment of residential construction and home ownership appears to be relatively neutral. Incentives such as premiums and tax privileges on savings for building purposes, accelerated depreciation schemes, individual housing allowances or other fiscal concessions are practically unheard of in Switzerland. Interest payments on mortgages are deductible from the taxable income of home-owners, who must nevertheless pay income tax on imputed rents. The tax provisions applicable to this rent *vary* from one canton to another.

81. Schulz, H.-R. *et al.* (1993), "Wohneigentumsförderung durch den Bund", *Bulletin du logement,* Vol. 55, Berne.

82. It should be noted, however, that advertised property prices have fallen considerably during the past two years: the prices of rental apartments have fallen by nearly 25 per cent, of detached houses by 18 per cent and of owner-occupied apartments by around 10 per cent. Wüest and Partner (1994), *Immobilienmarkt Schweiz.*

83. Reviewed in Farago, P., *et al.* (1993), "Comportement des investisseurs sur le marché immobilier du logement", *Bulletin du logement,* Vol. 54, Berne.

84. The Swiss will have to decide on the degree to which they want greater residential use of rural areas as opposed to more intensive residential use of urban zones. An important aspect of the redefinition of agricultural zones will be the degree of freedom offered to farmers to develop non-farm activities.

References

Aeberhardt, W., and M. Zumstein (1990), *Zinsinsel Schweiz,* Bundesamt für Konjunkturfragen, Study No. 13, Berne.

Ammann, Y. (1988), "Le budget de plein emploi", *Cahiers de conjoncture,* No. 2.

Banque nationale suisse (1992), "La politique monétaire suisse en 1993", *Monnaie et conjoncture,* Bulletin trimestriel de la Banque nationale suisse, December.

Banque nationale suisse (1993), "La politique monétaire suisse en 1994", *Monnaie et conjoncture,* Bulletin trimestriel de la Banque nationale suisse, December.

Banque nationale suisse, *86ᵉ rapport de gestion, 1994,* p. 10.

Commission suisse des cartels (1988), "Les soumissions et les achats de la Confédération, des cantons et de certaines communes", Report No. 2, Berne.

Commission suisse des cartels (1993), "L'état de concurrence sur le marché du ciment", Report No. 5, Berne.

Cornioley, C. (1994), "La situation des jeunes au chômage", *La Vie économique,* April.

Farago, P., *et al.* (1993), "Comportement des investisseurs sur le marché immobilier du logement", *Bulletin du logement,* Vol. 54, Berne.

Felder, S. and J. Finsinger (1987), "Auswirkungen protektionistischer und preisstützender Submissionsvorschriften auf die Baubranche", *Revue suisse d'économie politique et de statistique,* June.

Felder, S., *et al.* (1993), "The Swiss Construction Sector", in: Zweifel, P., *Services in Switzerland,* published by Springer-Verlag, Berlin.

Felder, S. (1994), "Auswirkungen der öffentlichen Vergabepolitik auf den Wettbewerbspreis in der Bauwirtschaft", *Swiss Journal of Economics and Statistics,* June.

Flückiger, H. (1989), "La bataille pour le sol – Défis lancés à l'aménagement du territoire", *La vie économique,* December.

Lambelet, J.-Chr. (1994), *Niveau de vie et niveau des prix en Suisse et dans les autres pays de l'OCDE,* CREA, Lausanne, April.

OECD, *Economic Survey of Switzerland,* various issues, Paris.

OECD, *1990/91 Economic Survey of Austria,* Paris.

Office fédéral du logement (1993), *Abaisser les coûts dans la construction de logements,* Rapport de travail sur le logement 27, Berne.

Office fédéral de statistiques (1994), *Les statistiques annuelles de la construction.*

Rapport sur l'aménagement du territoire, Berne, 1987.

Schips, B. and E. Müller (1993), "Mietzinsniveau bei Marktmieten", in: *Office fédéral du logement,* Materialien zum Bericht der Studienkommission Marktmiete, Rapport de travail sur le logement, Vol. 29, Berne.

Schulz, H.-R. *et al.* (1993), "Wohneigentumsförderung durch den Bund", *Bulletin du logement,* Vol. 55, Berne.

Wüest and Partner (1994), *Immobilienmarkt Schweiz.*

Annex

Calendar of main economic events

1993

January

The National Bank lowers the discount rate by $\frac{1}{2}$ percentage point to 5.5 per cent.

February

The Federal Council submits to Parliament the follow-up programme to the rejection of the EEA agreement. Three options for integration policy remain open: the deepening of bilateral relations, a later participation in the EEA and joining the EC. In current circumstances, the government gives priority to bilateral relations (sectoral contracts). Measures have been and will be taken to render Swiss laws compatible with European legislation. Of the adjustments of Swiss laws to EEA rules proposed to Parliament before 6 December 1992, more than half have been taken up again and are submitted to Parliament. The so-called "Swisslex" package of measures, however, only partly substitutes for the internal liberalisation measures foreseen under the EEA agreement. Consequently, other measures "favouring a revival of the market economy" are envisaged. In the course of 1993, reform projects will be prepared to further liberalise the labour market and the internal market for goods and services, to reform competition policy and to eliminate technical impediments to the flow of goods and services between cantons.

March

The Federal Council submits to Parliament a supplementary budget proposal for an extra expenditures of SF 1.4 billion, SF 1.3 billion of which are a loan to the unemployment insurance system. In addition, a proposal for an employment programme targeted at the construction sector is submitted for parliamentary approval. Of the total programme of SF 300 million, two-thirds is devoted to an "investment bonus" in the form of a federal subsidy of 15 to 20 per cent of the cost of infrastructure investment by municipalities and cantons.

The Swiss people endorse by referendum an increase in the customs duty on petrol by 20 centimes per litre.

The National Bank lowers the discount rate by $\frac{1}{2}$ percentage point to 5.0 per cent.

June

The Parliament adopts a draft law on the introduction of value-added tax (VAT), which will be subject to referendum in November 1993. In the case of approval by the people, the introduction of VAT is envisaged for 1 January 1995. Depending on the outcome of the referendum, the standard tax rate could be set at 6.2 or 6.5 per cent (a reduced rate of 1.9 per cent for certain goods and services). The draft law also foresees the possibility to set a lower VAT rate for certain services which are mainly consumed by foreign tourists. 5 per cent of the revenues from VAT are earmarked for transfers to the health insurance system in favour of low income groups. Moreover, the proposed law enables the Parliament to raise the VAT rate by up to 1 percentage point in order to finance the increased burden on the old-age and disability insurance resulting from the "ageing" of the population.

July

A new collective agreement in the machinery industry comes into effect until the end of 1995, which permits variations in working hours and reductions in wages in case of "economic difficulties and in order to improve the chances to maintain employment". Under certain conditions, the new agreement allows companies to shorten or lengthen working hours without wage compensation and to cut in part or even fully the payment of the thirteenth monthly salary.

The National Bank cuts its discount rate by $\frac{1}{2}$ percentage point to 4.5 per cent.

August

In the context of the "revitalisation programme", the Federal Council proposes to Parliament a modification to patent law aimed at strengthening research in Switzerland and abolishing the comparative disadvantages of Swiss industry in this domain.

September

The Swiss people approve a change in the law on unemployment insurance. For the next two years this envisages the reduction – under certain conditions – of unemployment benefits to 70 per cent of the insured salary and the extension of the payment period from 300 to 400 days.

October

The National Bank cuts the discount rate by $\frac{1}{4}$ percentage point to 4.25 per cent.

The Federal Council submits to Parliament a draft budget consolidation programme, which mainly consists of selective expenditure cuts. These are proposed to replace the across-the-board linear cuts decided in 1992, which are to expire at the end of 1995. It is the aim of the redressment package to curtail the federal structural budget deficit. The budgetary relief from the programme is estimated at SF 1½ billion per annum until 1997.

November

In a national referendum, the Swiss people and the cantons approve a Federal-Council proposal on the reform of the Confederation tax system. *Inter alia,* this encompasses the replacement of the current turnover tax on goods by a general value-added tax (VAT) as from 1995. The standard VAT rate is set at 6.5 per cent, 0.3 percentage point above the current turnover tax rate on goods, as a contribution to federal budget consolidation. The government is also given authority to raise the VAT rate by 1 percentage point to help finance the public pension scheme. The electorate also endorsed the conversion of the customs duties on automobiles and petrol into specific taxes.

The Federal Council submits to Parliament a revision of the law on unemployment insurance. The main features of the amendment are an increase in the unemployment insurance contribution rate from 2 to 3 per cent of salary, a rise in the maximum contributory gross salary by 150 per cent and higher transfers from the Confederation and cantons to the unemployment insurance fund. It is proposed to make permanent earlier temporary cuts in unemployment benefits and the extended duration of benefit payments. Further elements of the proposal are the re-introduction of a descending scale of daily benefit, the extension of active labour market policies, the widening of the definition of a reasonable job offer to benefit recipients and enforced measures against the abuse of the unemployment insurance.

December

Parliament adopts the 1994 budget of the Confederation, which foresees expenditures growing by 4.9 per cent and revenues by 8.6 per cent. This is projected to bring the federal deficit down from an actual SF 7.8 billion in 1993 to SF 7.0 billion in 1994, about 2 per cent of GDP.

The National Bank lowers the discount rate by ¼ percentage point to 4.0 per cent.

The National Bank decides to adhere in 1994 to its policy of aiming at annual average growth in the monetary base of 1 per cent during a period of five years.

Parliament endorses a draft law on the portability of old-age, survivor and invalidity pensions.

Parliament approves a draft law on the use of pension funds by the insured for the financing of owner-occupied housing.

An agreement is reached between Switzerland and the member states of the European Economic Area exempting bilaterally traded goods from duty.

1994

February

In a national referendum, the people and the cantons approve a constitutional amendment on the continuation of the motorway toll (the "vignette") and on a special levy on lorries to 2004. Moreover, Swiss voters endorse a popular initiative which aims at banning transalpine freight trucks and making freight transit by rail compulsory. The initiative gives transport companies and governments ten years before these restrictions take effect. The proposal also bans road construction which would boost transit capacity.

April

The National Bank lowers the discount rate from 4.0 to 3.5 per cent.

STATISTICAL AND STRUCTURAL ANNEX

Selected background statistics

	Average 1983-93	1984	1985	1986	1987	1988	1989	1990	1991	1992	1993
A. Percentage change from previous year at constant 1980 prices											
Private consumption	1.4	1.6	1.4	2.8	2.1	2.1	2.2	1.5	1.5	-0.2	-0.8
Gross fixed capital formation	2.8	4.1	5.3	7.9	7.4	6.9	5.8	2.6	-2.5	-5.0	-4.3
Construction	2.2	4.1	3.0	4.2	5.4	6.4	6.9	1.9	-3.1	-2.3	-4.2
Machinery and equipment	4.2	4.3	10.4	15.4	11.3	7.9	3.9	3.7	-1.2	-9.6	-4.3
GDP	1.9	1.8	3.7	2.9	2.0	2.9	3.9	2.3	0.0	-0.1	-0.6
GDP price deflator	3.5	2.8	3.1	3.8	2.6	2.4	4.2	5.7	5.5	2.6	2.5
Industrial production	2.7	3.6	5.0	3.9	0.6	8.9	2.6	2.7	0.5	-0.7	-0.5
Employment	0.4	1.0	1.9	1.4	1.2	1.2	1.1	1.3	-0.1	-2.2	-2.6
Compensation of employees (current prices)	5.4	4.1	6.0	6.1	4.9	5.9	6.9	8.9	7.3	3.4	0.5
Productivity (real GDP/employment)	1.5	0.8	1.7	1.5	0.9	1.7	2.7	1.0	0.1	2.2	2.1
Unit labour cost (compensation/real GDP)	3.5	2.3	2.2	3.1	2.8	2.9	2.9	6.4	7.4	3.4	1.1
B. Percentage ratios											
Gross fixed capital formation as per cent of GDP at constant prices	27.7	25.0	25.4	26.6	28.0	29.1	29.6	29.7	29.0	27.6	26.5
Stockbuilding as per cent of GDP at constant prices	1.2	0.7	0.6	2.0	2.3	1.4	2.0	2.1	1.2	-0.5	-0.3
Foreign balance as per cent of GDP at constant prices	-4.5	-3.0	-1.8	-4.5	-6.2	-6.1	-6.3	-6.3	-5.8	-2.7	-1.8
Compensation of employees as per cent of GDP at current prices	60.8	61.2	60.7	60.3	60.4	60.7	60.0	60.4	61.5	62.0	61.1
Direct taxes as per cent of household disposable income	17.9	18.3	18.1	18.8	17.9	18.1	17.5	18.0	17.2	17.7	17.9
Household saving as per cent of disposable income	9.9	5.8	5.7	7.0	8.4	10.0	10.9	12.2	13.0	13.1	13.2
Unemployment as per cent of total labour force	1.3	1.1	0.9	0.8	0.7	0.6	0.5	0.5	1.1	2.5	4.5
C. Other indicators											
Current balance ($ billion)	9.3	4.4	5.0	6.9	7.6	9.0	7.0	8.6	10.6	15.0	18.6

Source: OECD, National Accounts.

Table A. **Gross national product**

Million Swiss francs, current prices

	1984	1985	1986	1987	1988	1989	1990	1991	1992	1993
Private consumption	133 610	140 555	144 925	150 210	156 970	166 150	177 650	190 490	197 915	201 945
Public consumption[1]	28 925	30 880	32 325	33 025	35 405	38 485	42 850	46 640	49 665	51 345
Gross fixed asset formation	49 800	54 200	58 995	64 370	71 480	79 860	84 545	84 810	80 375	75 615
Change in stocks[2]	1 600	1 365	4 370	4 975	3 355	6 435	7 310	4 545	-550	225
Domestic demand	213 935	227 000	240 615	252 580	267 210	290 930	312 355	326 485	327 405	329 130
Exports of goods and services	80 450	89 015	89 115	90 525	97 990	110 510	115 050	116 720	122 245	124 770
Imports of goods and services	81 155	88 065	86 380	88 420	96 790	111 080	113 415	112 130	110 180	107 800
Gross domestic product at market prices	213 230	227 950	243 350	254 685	268 410	290 360	313 990	331 075	339 470	346 100
Factor income from abroad	19 795	21 250	20 595	20 900	24 185	28 010	28 130	28 740	27 490	29 560
less: Factor income paid abroad	6 965	7 845	9 020	9 495	9 645	13 200	14 535	14 965	14 215	15 060
Gross national product at market prices	226 060	241 355	254 925	266 090	282 950	305 170	327 585	345 390	352 745	360 600

1. Includes private social security.
2. Including statistical discrepancy.
Source: Office fédéral de la statistique.

Table B. Gross national product
Million Swiss francs, 1980 prices

	1984	1985	1986	1987	1988	1989	1990	1991	1992	1993
Private consumption	112 060	113 665	116 870	119 290	121 845	124 560	126 430	128 285	128 015	126 960
Public consumption[1]	23 955	24 735	25 650	26 115	27 235	28 365	29 695	30 150	30 315	30 205
Gross fixed asset formation	43 935	46 260	49 910	53 620	57 340	60 650	62 210	60 685	57 640	55 185
Change in stocks[2]	1 290	1 155	3 805	4 335	2 715	4 105	4 335	2 455	-1 139	-570
Domestic demand	181 240	185 815	196 235	203 360	209 135	217 680	222 670	221 575	214 831	211 780
Exports of goods and services	68 480	74 170	74 445	75 695	80 090	84 090	86 630	86 005	88 900	89 625
Imports of goods and services	73 760	77 500	82 965	87 530	92 145	97 080	99 905	98 245	94 520	93 385
Gross domestic product at market prices	175 960	182 485	187 715	191 525	197 080	204 690	209 395	209 335	209 211	208 020
Factor income from abroad	18 025	18 935	17 665	17 415	18 810	19 520	20 570	19 855	17 520	18 200
less: Factor income paid abroad	6 260	7 185	8 790	9 475	9 180	12 200	12 620	11 985	10 710	11 000
Gross national product at market prices	187 725	194 235	196 590	199 465	206 710	212 010	217 345	217 205	216 021	215 220

1. Includes private social security.
2. Including statistical discrepancy.
Source: Office fédéral de la statistique.

126

Table C. **Producer and import prices**

May 1993 = 100

	1992	1993 [1]	1993 Q2 [2]	1993 Q3	1993 Q4	1994 Q1
Producer price index						
Total	99.5	99.9	100.1	100.1	99.5	99.3
Agricultural products		101.9	100.9	102.7	101.7	101.9
Manufacturing	99.5	99.7	99.0	99.9	99.2	99.0
Food and tobacco		100.3	100.3	100.8	99.7	100.1
Textiles and clothing		100.0	100.0	100.1	100.0	99.9
Paper and paper products		98.9	100.0	99.2	97.8	97.5
Petroleum products		96.7	98.4	96.2	96.1	90.6
Chemicals		99.2	100.0	99.7	98.2	96.7
Machinery		99.9	100.0	100.0	99.8	99.8
Transport equipment		100.4	100.0	100.0	101.1	101.1
Furniture and other articles		101.9	100.3	102.5	102.4	103.1
Electricity and gas		100.4	100.0	100.0	101.0	101.2
Domestic market		100.0	100.1	100.3	99.7	99.7
Exports		99.7	100.0	99.9	99.2	98.9
Raw materials		103.3	101.1	104.1	103.9	105.5
Semi-finished goods		99.6	100.1	99.9	99.0	98.6
Consumer goods		99.8	100.0	99.9	99.7	99.7
Capital goods		99.9	100.0	100.0	99.7	99.7
Import price index	100.2	99.8	100.0	99.9	99.5	98.9
Raw materials		104.8	100.3	105.5	107.2	110.0
Semi-finished goods		99.6	99.9	99.9	99.0	98.4
Consumer goods		99.9	99.9	99.9	100.0	98.9
Capital goods		98.4	99.3	98.6	97.8	97.0
Total supply price	99.7	99.9	100.0	100.1	99.5	99.2
Raw materials		103.8	100.8	104.6	105.1	107.2
Semi-finished goods		99.6	100.0	99.9	99.0	98.6
Consumer goods		99.9	99.9	99.9	99.8	99.4
Capital goods		99.3	99.7	99.5	99.0	98.7

1. As from May 1993, the wholesale price index has been replaced by the total supply price index, which is the total of the producer price and the import price indices. Therefore indices for 1993 are the averages for May to December.
2. Indices for Q2 are the averages for May and June 1993.
Source: Office fédéral de la statistique.

Table D. **Money supply**

Million Swiss francs, yearly average

	1984	1985	1986	1987	1988	1989	1990	1991	1992	1993
Monetary base	30 484	31 142	31 768	32 708	31 420	29 925	28 898	29 274	29 020	29 525
Money supply M1	63 140	63 210	66 354	71 351	81 480	77 032	73 775	74 687	74 798	83 401
Money supply M2	111 095	119 182	126 168	138 502	149 097	179 036	202 337	208 882	210 168	195 675
Money supply M3	247 605	259 599	277 146	303 392	333 089	353 719	362 145	373 669	384 230	404 802

Source: Banque nationale suisse, *Bulletin mensuel.*

Table E. Interest rates and capital markets

Million Swiss francs and percentages

	1990	1991	1992	1993	1992 Q1	Q2	Q3	Q4	1993 Q1	Q2	Q3	Q4	1994 Q1	Q2
Interest rates (average for the period)														
Discount rate (end of period)	6.0	7.0	6.0	4.0	7.0	7.0	6.0	6.0	5.0	5.0	4.5	4.0	4.0	3.5
Three-months deposits (Zurich)	8.3	7.6	7.2	4.3	7.4	8.6	7.2	5.7	4.8	4.5	4.1	3.8	3.5	3.6
Government bond yield	6.4	6.2	6.4	4.6	6.3	6.8	6.7	5.8	5.0	4.7	4.4	4.1	4.3	4.9
Savings deposits of cantonal banks	4.6	5.1	5.1	4.4	5.1	5.1	5.1	5.1	5.1	4.6	4.1	3.9	3.5	3.4
Memorandum items:														
Euro-dollar, three-month	8.2	5.9	3.8	3.2	4.2	4.0	3.3	3.6	3.2	3.1	3.1	3.3	3.5	4.4
Euro-bond yields (dollars)	9.3	8.2	6.8	6.1	6.9	7.3	6.3	6.5	6.5	6.1	5.9	5.8	5.8	7.1
Capital market														
Foreign bonds	32 095	31 931	25 196	45 121	6 468	3 747	3 905	11 077	8 601	9 924	13 379	13 217	15 434	
Domestic bonds	18 234	17 631	25 793	34 909	8 101	5 328	5 217	7 147	14 190	3 149	8 723	8 845	9 385	
Public market issues[1]	17 146	16 202	24 558	32 757	7 512	5 119	5 109	6 818	12 939	3 021	8 529	8 267	9 298	
of which: Government	3 340	4 332	12 286	15 793	3 679	2 167	3 118	3 322	5 841	1 825	4 064	4 064	4 684	
Financial Institutions[2]	11 068	9 663	8 624	11 786	2 208	2 230	1 384	2 801	4 915	723	2 718	3 431	3 214	
Other private	2 739	2 207	3 648	5 178	1 625	722	607	695	2 184	473	1 747	773	1 399	
Shares														
Public market issues	3 356	1 899	2 598	3 286	668	845	697	388	102	537	1 610	1 037	1 076	
Redemptions	10 223	11 419	18 474	30 205	5 127	4 150	3 358	5 840	6 631	7 126	6 613	9 835	9 357	

1. According to date of payment.
2. Including holding companies.
Source: Banque nationale suisse, *Bulletin mensuel*, and OECD, *Financial Statistics*.

Table F. **Foreign trade by area**

Million US dollars

	1984	1985	1986	1987	1988	1989	1990	1991	1992	1993
Exports, fob										
OECD countries	19 739.8	20 914.9	29 310.8	35 867.3	40 165.8	41 003.5	50 929.7	49 212.4	52 362.0	49 242.4
EEC	13 711.7	14 337.1	20 570.8	25 465.3	28 684.9	29 399.7	36 899.3	36 078.0	38 607.0	35 792.2
EFTA	1 936.9	2 039.2	2 820.5	3 335.2	3 540.2	3 422.8	4 221.7	3 952.4	4 133.6	3 999.6
United States	2 551.6	2 831.5	3 560.1	4 004.9	4 344.4	4 589.5	5 079.7	5 038.1	5 593.0	5 635.9
Other	1 539.6	1 707.1	2 359.3	3 061.9	3 596.2	3 591.4	4 729.0	4 143.8	4 028.4	3 814.7
Non-OECD countries	6 073.8	6 201.3	7 936.2	9 382.9	10 448.3	10 506.0	12 601.2	12 117.5	13 169.2	13 892.0
CEEC	723.4	802.1	1 014.0	1 283.3	1 388.8	1 450.6	1 657.0	1 698.1	1 621.8	1 639.8
OPEC	1 827.5	1 604.9	1 697.0	1 888.0	1 988.7	1 591.9	1 979.0	2 077.8	2 364.6	2 443.2
Other	3 522.9	3 794.3	5 225.2	6 211.5	7 070.8	7 463.4	8 965.2	8 341.6	9 182.8	9 809.0
Total	25 813.6	27 116.2	37 246.9	45 250.2	50 614.1	51 509.4	63 531.0	61 329.8	65 531.2	63 134.4
Imports, cif										
OECD countries	25 478.5	26 790.9	37 155.3	45 428.5	50 627.4	52 380.4	62 673.9	59 379.6	59 518.6	54 938.4
EEC	20 328.6	21 577.7	29 909.6	36 447.3	40 220.9	41 312.2	49 841.4	46 514.5	47 399.8	44 129.0
EFTA	1 856.7	1 966.3	2 796.7	3 562.8	4 036.9	4 219.6	5 010.7	4 593.7	4 526.6	4 075.4
United States	1 949.4	1 791.2	2 212.0	2 686.5	3 124.5	3 722.5	4 269.0	4 867.2	4 190.9	3 921.0
Other	1 343.8	1 455.6	2 236.9	2 732.0	3 245.0	3 126.1	3 552.9	3 404.2	3 401.3	2 812.9
Non-OECD countries	3 897.4	3 647.0	3 709.7	4 981.4	5 682.8	5 817.4	6 871.4	6 891.2	6 146.9	5 855.3
CEEC	865.5	804.9	745.5	654.3	598.5	654.3	683.1	922.2	795.5	767.8
OPEC	959.0	973.9	614.8	715.4	604.4	327.6	851.5	912.0	655.8	720.5
Other	2 073.0	1 868.1	2 349.4	3 611.7	4 480.0	4 835.4	5 336.8	5 057.0	4 695.6	4 367.0
Total	29 375.9	30 437.9	40 865.0	50 409.9	56 310.2	58 197.7	69 545.4	66 270.9	65 665.4	60 793.7

Source: OECD, *Foreign Trade Statistics*, Series A.

Table G. Foreign trade by commodity group

Million US dollars

	1984	1985	1986	1987	1988	1989	1990	1991	1992	1993
Exports, fob										
0. Food and live animals	687	731	982	1 154	1 144	1 142	1 407	1 392	1 493	1 497
1. Beverages and tobacco	155	138	188	228	258	255	359	377	416	396
2. Crude materials, inedible, except fuels	384	383	457	526	664	678	740	671	706	655
3. Mineral fuels, lubricants and related materials	91	91	65	62	69	57	83	127	104	116
4. Animal and vegetable oils and fats	18	18	17	19	18	20	24	23	22	20
5. Chemicals	5 503	5 879	8 137	9 976	11 045	10 912	13 653	13 476	15 303	15 658
6. Manufactured goods, classified chiefly by material	5 462	5 572	7 370	8 732	10 101	10 211	12 352	11 362	11 654	11 081
7. Machinery and transport equipment	7 725	8 546	12 249	15 045	16 436	16 066	20 519	19 360	20 049	18 752
8. Miscellaneous manufactured articles	5 567	5 892	8 095	9 548	10 625	11 739	15 386	14 242	15 451	15 694
9. Commodities and transactions, not classified according to kind	39	35	36	72	271	360	476	446	417	469
Total	25 631	27 285	37 596	45 362	50 631	51 440	64 999	61 477	65 615	64 338
Imports, cif										
0. Food and live animals	1 912	1 949	2 536	2 960	3 037	2 859	3 399	3 381	3 453	3 318
1. Beverages and tobacco	360	392	531	651	715	726	906	884	833	785
2. Crude materials, inedible, except fuels	1 030	1 039	1 273	1 484	1 644	1 672	1 896	1 637	1 613	1 470
3. Mineral fuels, lubricants and related materials	3 030	3 074	2 421	2 252	2 086	2 318	3 235	3 105	2 838	2 447
4. Animal and vegetable oils and fats	59	64	66	56	55	54	69	62	73	77
5. Chemicals	3 397	3 665	4 798	5 721	6 675	6 617	7 954	7 617	8 332	8 324
6. Manufactured goods, classified chiefly by material	6 435	6 476	8 993	10 994	12 291	13 270	15 412	13 766	13 306	12 781
7. Machinery and transport equipment	7 274	7 974	12 225	15 975	18 187	18 250	22 353	21 122	20 213	18 321
8. Miscellaneous manufactured articles	5 655	5 822	8 275	10 415	11 443	11 991	14 900	14 235	14 480	13 819
9. Commodities and transactions, not classified according to kind	168	179	80	50	192	379	520	480	462	508
Total	29 320	30 634	41 198	50 558	56 325	58 136	70 644	66 288	65 603	61 850

Source: OECD, *Foreign Trade Statistics*, Series C.

Table H. Balance of payments

Million US dollars

	1984	1985	1986	1987	1988	1989	1990	1991	1992	1993
Exports, fob	26 785	28 100	38 470	46 685	52 258	53 182	65 594	63 373	67 799	65 487
Imports, cif[1]	29 084	30 070	40 456	49 789	55 449	57 304	68 834	65 509	65 060	60 448
Trade balance	-2 299	-1 970	-1 986	-3 104	-3 191	-4 122	-3 240	-2 136	2 739	5 039
Services, net	7 503	7 812	9 943	12 165	13 948	12 828	14 206	15 325	15 286	16 349
of which: Investment income	6 710	6 753	8 499	10 506	13 343	12 691	14 756	15 287	14 783	14 709
Other factor income	-1 250	-1 299	-2 063	-2 855	-3 407	-3 635	-4 966	-5 310		
Balance on goods and services	5 204	5 842	7 957	9 061	10 757	8 706	10 966	13 189	18 025	21 388
Private transfers, net	-825	-840	-1 206	-1 549	-1 712	-1 666	-2 184	-2 275	-2 369	-2 195
Official transfers, net	-9	34	116	45	-2	-18	-146	-346	-609	-564
Current balance	4 370	5 036	6 867	7 557	9 043	7 022	8 636	10 568	15 047	18 629
Balance on non-monetary transactions	2 127	704	5 757	4 294	-8 941	-16 910	-9 183	-4 088	9 051	
Private monetary institutions'										
short-term capital	-628	467	-4 704	-1 164	6 578	18 388	10 386	5 052	-4 628	
Assets (– = increase)	-849	-4 881	-10 167	-13 407	3 174	8 854	-2 125	1 984	-4 616	
Liabilities	221	5 348	5 463	12 243	3 404	9 534	12 511	3 068	-12	
Balance on official settlements [2]	1 499	1 171	1 053	3 130	-2 363	1 478	1 203	964	4 423	
Special transactions	..	..	..	..	..	..	..	..	..	
Miscellaneous official accounts	2	-1 456	-2 045	-2 284	1 361	839	-2 929	1 154	408	
Change in reserves (+ = increase)	2 630	-284	-992	846	-1 001	2 316	-1 727	2 111	4 829	
Gold	..	..	..	..	..	..	..	..	..	
Currency assets[3]	2 668	-126	-773	1 071	-884	2 344	-1 672	2 108	4 002	
Reserve position in IMF	-35	-152	-215	-237	-125	-86	-47	..	814	
Special Drawing Rights	-3	-7	-4	12	8	57	-8	3	13	

1. Imports cif minus 5 per cent as estimate for freight and insurance.
2. Central Bank liabilities and other assets.
3. Including Roosa-bonds held by the Confederation.
Source: Banque national suisse, *Bulletin mensuel*, and OECD estimates.

132

Table I. **Gross value added by main area of activity**

	SF millions			As a percentage of GDP		
	1975	1985	1990	1975	1985	1990
Enterprises	124 685	203 930	280 051	89.0	89.5	89.2
Non-financial enterprises	116 282	180 832	250 681	83.0	79.3	79.8
Agriculture, forestry	6 487	8 180	9 664	4.6	3.6	3.1
Energy, metal ore mining	2 808	5 023	6 011	2.0	2.2	1.9
Industrial arts and crafts	41 687	58 794	76 722	29.7	25.8	24.4
Building and civil engineering	11 210	17 325	26 224	8.0	7.6	8.4
Distributive trades, hotels and catering, repairs	29 430	44 689	62 343	21.0	19.6	19.9
Transport and communications	9 140	14 550	18 556	6.5	6.4	5.9
Real estate and consultancy services	5 946	15 100	26 324	4.2	6.6	8.4
Rental and dwellings	5 290	9 878	13 949	3.8	4.3	4.4
Other services	4 284	7 293	10 887	3.1	3.2	3.5
Banking and insurance	8 403	23 096	29 370	6.0	10.1	9.4
Government and social insurance	14 452	26 065	37 070	10.3	11.4	11.8
Household and private non-profit institutions	2 453	4 655	6 783	1.8	2.0	2.2
Total (unadjusted)	141 590	234 650	323 903	101.1	102.9	103.2
Adjustments						
Imputed value of bank service charge	-4 565	-10 400	-14 180	-3.3	-4.6	-4.5
Import duties	3 130	3 700	4 267	2.2	1.6	1.4
Adjusted total = gross domestic product	140 155	227 950	313 990	100.0	100.0	100.0

Source: Office fédéral de la statistique, *National Accounts.*

Table J. Labour market: structural and institutional characteristics

	1975	1980	1985	1989	1990	1991	1992	1993
Labour force (thousand)	3 118	3 172	3 382	3 535	3 583	3 600	3 573	3 552
of which: Foreigners,[1] end-August	754	706	756	904	955	989	977	950
Participation rate[2] (per cent)								
Total	74.8	74.4	75.5	77.6	78.1	77.6	76.3	75.4
Male	97.7	94.5	94.4	96.2	96.4	95.4	93.9	92.8
Female	51.9	54.1	56.2	58.8	59.7	59.7	58.6	57.9
Employment/labour force	74.5	74.2	74.5	77.0	77.6	76.8	74.3	71.9
Employment by sector								
Agriculture	7.6	6.9	6.1	5.6	5.6	5.5	5.6	5.6
Industry	42.2	38.1	35.6	35.1	35.0	34.4	33.9	33.2
Services	50.2	55.0	58.3	59.3	59.5	60.1	60.5	61.2
Wholly unemployed	..	6 255	27 024	15 133	15 980	35 065	82 429	144 983
of which: Foreigners (per cent of total)	..	..	33.1	41.1	42.7	44.3	40.9	40.2
Unemployment rate	0.3	0.2	1.0	0.6	0.5	1.1	2.5	4.5
Vacancies: Full-time[3]	..	12 312	7 875	17 007	16 711	10 145	7 741	5 370
Part-time	..	..	647	545	550	404	425	373
Number of days not worked (lock-out and strikes)	1 733	5 178	662	265	4 090	51	673	0

1. Includes settled workers, workers on a one-year contract and seasonal and border workers.
2. Labour force as a percentage of the corresponding population aged 15-64.
3. The decomposition between full- and part-time begins in 1983, so for 1980 it is total vacancies.
Source: Office fédéral de la statistique, Annuaire statistique de la Suisse, 1993; Département fédéral de l'économie publique, La vie économique, and OECD, Labour Force Statistics.

Table K. **The structure of taxation**
Per cent of GDP

	1980	1985	1988	1989	1990	1991	1992	1993
The structure of taxation (per cent of GDP)								
Tax receipts	30.8	32.0	32.6	31.7	31.5	31.2	32.0	32.5
Personal income tax	11.0	11.2	11.1	10.6	10.8	10.7	11.1	10.6
Corporate tax	1.8	1.9	2.2	2.0	2.1	2.0	2.0	2.1
Social security tax	9.5	10.3	10.4	10.4	10.4	10.7	11.2	12.0
Property taxes	2.2	2.6	2.7	2.8	2.5	2.2	2.3	2.4
Consumption tax	5.8	5.6	5.7	5.5	5.4	5.2	5.0	5.1
Memorandum:								
Income tax as a per cent of total tax	41.4	40.9	40.8	39.9	41.0	40.7	41.0	38.9

Source: OECD, Revenue Statistics of OECD Member Countries, 1965-1993.

Table L. **Interest rate margins in banking**[1]

Per cent of average balance sheet total

	1981	1987	1988	1989	1990	1991	1992
Large banks	1.10	1.26	1.36	1.37	1.24	1.52	1.68
Cantonal banks	1.00	1.10	1.13	1.13	1.22	1.34	1.34
Regional and saving banks	1.30	1.18	1.21	1.20	1.32	1.48	1.51
Loans associations and agricultural credit co-operatives	1.00	0.94	0.95	0.96	1.04	1.13	1.14
Other Swiss and foreign banks	2.00	1.82	1.98	2.05	2.01	2.11	2.13

1. Interest received less interest paid.
Source: OECD, *Bank Profitability (Statistical Supplement), Financial Statements of Banks, 1983-92,* 1994.

BASIC STATISTICS:

INTERNATIONAL COMPARISONS

	Units	Reference period[1]	Australia	A
Population				
Total	Thousands	1991	17 292	7 8
Inhabitants per sq. km	Number	1991	2	
Net average annual increase over previous 10 years	%	1991	1.5	
Employment				
Total civilian employment (TCE)[2]	Thousands	1991	7 705	3 4
Of which: Agriculture	% of TCE		5.5	
Industry	% of TCE		24.2	3
Services	% of TCE		70.4	5
Gross domestic product (GDP)				
At current prices and current exchange rates	Bill. US$	1991	297.4	16
Per capita	US$		17 200	21
At current prices using current PPP's[3]	Bill. US$	1991	280	13
Per capita	US$		16 195	17 3
Average annual volume growth over previous 5 years	%	1991	2.8	
Gross fixed capital formation (GFCF)	% of GDP	1991	20.5	2
Of which: Machinery and equipment	% of GDP		8.8	1
Residential construction	% of GDP		4.6	
Average annual volume growth over previous 5 years	%	1991	0.3	
Gross saving ratio[4]	% of GDP	1991	17.2	2
General government				
Current expenditure on goods and services	% of GDP	1991	18.3	1
Current disbursements[5]	% of GDP	1991	36.6	4
Current receipts	% of GDP	1991	33.7	4
Net official development assistance	% of GDP	1991	0.35	0.
Indicators of living standards				
Private consumption per capita using current PPP's[3]	US$	1991	9 827	9 5
Passenger cars, per 1 000 inhabitants	Number	1990	430	3
Telephones, per 1 000 inhabitants	Number	1990	448 (89)	5
Television sets, per 1 000 inhabitants	Number	1989	484	4
Doctors, per 1 000 inhabitants	Number	1991	2	2
Infant mortality per 1 000 live births	Number	1991	7.1	7
Wages and prices (average annual increase over previous 5 years)				
Wages (earnings or rates according to availability)	%	1991	5.4	5
Consumer prices	%	1991	6.7	2
Foreign trade				
Exports of goods, fob*	Mill. US$	1991	39 764	40 9
As % of GDP	%		13.4	24
Average annual increase over previous 5 years	%		13.2	12
Imports of goods, cif*	Mill. US$	1991	38 844	48 9
As % of GDP	%		13.1	29
Average annual increase over previous 5 years	%		10.1	13
Total official reserves[6]	Mill. SDR's	1991	11 432	6 5
As ratio of average monthly imports of goods	Ratio		3.5	1

* At current prices and exchange rates.
1. Unless otherwise stated.
2. According to the definitions used in OECD *Labour Force Statistics*.
3. PPP's = Purchasing Power Parities.
4. Gross saving = Gross national disposable income minus private and government consumption.
5. Current disbursements = Current expenditure on goods and services plus current transfers and payments of property income.
6. Gold included in reserves is valued at 35 SDR's per ounce. End of year.
7. Including Luxembourg.

EMPLOYMENT OPPORTUNITIES

Economics Department, OECD

The Economics Department of the OECD offers challenging and rewarding opportunities to economists interested in applied policy analysis in an international environment. The Department's concerns extend across the entire field of economic policy analysis, both macro-economic and micro-economic. Its main task is to provide, for discussion by committees of senior officials from Member countries, documents and papers dealing with current policy concerns. Within this programme of work, three major responsibilities are:

- to prepare regular surveys of the economies of individual Member countries;
- to issue full twice-yearly reviews of the economic situation and prospects of the OECD countries in the context of world economic trends;
- to analyse specific policy issues in a medium-term context for theOECD as a whole, and to a lesser extent for the non-OECD countries.

The documents prepared for these purposes, together with much of the Department's other economic work, appear in published form in the *OECD Economic Outlook, OECD Economic Surveys, OECD Economic Studies* and the Department's *Working Papers* series.

The Department maintains a world econometric model, INTERLINK, which plays an important role in the preparation of the policy analyses and twice-yearly projections. The availability of extensive cross-country data bases and good computer resources facilitates comparative empirical analysis, much of which is incorporated into the model.

The Department is made up of about 75 professional economists from a variety of backgrounds and Member countries. Most projects are carried out by small teams and last from four to eighteen months. Within the Department, ideas and points of view are widely discussed; there is a lively professional interchange, and all professional staff have the opportunity to contribute actively to the programme of work.

Skills the Economics Department is looking for:

a) Solid competence in using the tools of both micro-economic and macro-economic theory to answer policy questions. Experience indicates that this normally requires the equivalent of a PH.D. in economics or substantial relevant professional experience to compensate for a lower degree.

b) Solid knowledge of economic statistics and quantitative methods; this includes how to identify data, estimate structural relationships, apply basic techniques of time series analysis, and test hypotheses. It is essential to be able to interpret results sensibly in an economic policy context.

c) A keen interest in and knowledge of policy issues, economic developments and their political/social contexts.

d) Interest and experience in analysing questions posed by policy-makers and presenting the results to them effectively and judiciously. Thus, work experience in government agencies or policy research institutions is an advantage.

e) The ability to write clearly, effectively, and to the point. The OECD is a bilingual organisation with French and English as the official languages. Candidates must have excellent knowledge of one of these languages, and some knowledge of the other. Knowledge of other languages might also be an advantage for certain posts.

f) For some posts, expertise in a particular area may be important, but a successful candidate is expected to be able to work on a broader range of topics relevant to the work of the Department. Thus, except in rare cases, the Department does not recruit narrow specialists.

g) The Department works on a tight time schedule and strict deadlines. Moreover, much of the work in the Department is carried out in small groups of economists. Thus, the ability to work with other economists from a variety of cultural and professional backgrounds, to supervise junior staff, and to produce work on time is important.

General Information

The salary for recruits depends on educational and professional background. Positions carry a basic salary from FF 262 512 or FF 323 916 for Administrators (economists) and from FF 375 708 for Principal Administrators (senior economists). This may be supplemented by expatriation and/or family allowances, depending on nationality, residence and family situation. Initial appointments are for a fixed term of two to three years.

Vacancies are open to candidates from OECD Member countries. The Organisation seeks to maintain an appropriate balance between female and male staff and among nationals from Member countries.

For further information on employment opportunities in the Economics Department, contact:

Administrative Unit
Economics Department
OECD
2, rue André-Pascal
75775 PARIS CEDEX 16
FRANCE

Applications citing "ECSUR", together with a detailed *curriculum vitae* in English or French, should be sent to the Head of Personnel at the above address.

MAIN SALES OUTLETS OF OECD PUBLICATIONS
PRINCIPAUX POINTS DE VENTE DES PUBLICATIONS DE L'OCDE

ARGENTINA – ARGENTINE
Carlos Hirsch S.R.L.
Galería Güemes, Florida 165, 4° Piso
1333 Buenos Aires   Tel. (1) 331.1787 y 331.2391
Telefax: (1) 331.1787

AUSTRALIA – AUSTRALIE
D.A. Information Services
648 Whitehorse Road, P.O.B 163
Mitcham, Victoria 3132   Tel. (03) 873.4411
Telefax: (03) 873.5679

AUSTRIA – AUTRICHE
Gerold & Co.
Graben 31
Wien I   Tel. (0222) 533.50.14

BELGIUM – BELGIQUE
Jean De Lannoy
Avenue du Roi 202
B-1060 Bruxelles   Tel. (02) 538.51.69/538.08.41
Telefax: (02) 538.08.41

CANADA
Renouf Publishing Company Ltd.
1294 Algoma Road
Ottawa, ON K1B 3W8   Tel. (613) 741.4333
Telefax: (613) 741.5439
Stores:
61 Sparks Street
Ottawa, ON K1P 5R1   Tel. (613) 238.8985
211 Yonge Street
Toronto, ON M5B 1M4   Tel. (416) 363.3171
Telefax: (416)363.59.63
Les Éditions La Liberté Inc.
3020 Chemin Sainte-Foy
Sainte-Foy, PQ G1X 3V6   Tel. (418) 658.3763
Telefax: (418) 658.3763
Federal Publications Inc.
165 University Avenue, Suite 701
Toronto, ON M5H 3B8   Tel. (416) 860.1611
Telefax: (416) 860.1608
Les Publications Fédérales
1185 Université
Montréal, QC H3B 3A7   Tel. (514) 954.1633
Telefax : (514) 954.1635

CHINA – CHINE
China National Publications Import
Export Corporation (CNPIEC)
16 Gongti E. Road, Chaoyang District
P.O. Box 88 or 50
Beijing 100704 PR   Tel. (01) 506.6688
Telefax: (01) 506.3101

DENMARK – DANEMARK
Munksgaard Book and Subscription Service
35, Nørre Søgade, P.O. Box 2148
DK-1016 København K   Tel. (33) 12.85.70
Telefax: (33) 12.93.87

FINLAND – FINLANDE
Akateeminen Kirjakauppa
Keskuskatu 1, P.O. Box 128
00100 Helsinki
Subscription Services/Agence d'abonnements :
P.O. Box 23
00371 Helsinki   Tel. (358 0) 12141
Telefax: (358 0) 121.4450

FRANCE
OECD/OCDE
Mail Orders/Commandes par correspondance:
2, rue André-Pascal
75775 Paris Cedex 16   Tel. (33-1) 45.24.82.00
Telefax: (33-1) 49.10.42.76
Telex: 640048 OCDE

OECD Bookshop/Librairie de l'OCDE :
33, rue Octave-Feuillet
75016 Paris   Tel. (33-1) 45.24.81.67
(33-1) 45.24.81.81
Documentation Française
29, quai Voltaire
75007 Paris   Tel. 40.15.70.00
Gibert Jeune (Droit-Économie)
6, place Saint-Michel
75006 Paris   Tel. 43.25.91.19
Librairie du Commerce International
10, avenue d'Iéna
75016 Paris   Tel. 40.73.34.60
Librairie Dunod
Université Paris-Dauphine
Place du Maréchal de Lattre de Tassigny
75016 Paris   Tel. (1) 44.05.40.13
Librairie Lavoisier
11, rue Lavoisier
75008 Paris   Tel. 42.65.39.95
Librairie L.G.D.J. - Montchrestien
20, rue Soufflot
75005 Paris   Tel. 46.33.89.85
Librairie des Sciences Politiques
30, rue Saint-Guillaume
75007 Paris   Tel. 45.48.36.02
P.U.F.
49, boulevard Saint-Michel
75005 Paris   Tel. 43.25.83.40
Librairie de l'Université
12a, rue Nazareth
13100 Aix-en-Provence   Tel. (16) 42.26.18.08
Documentation Française
165, rue Garibaldi
69003 Lyon   Tel. (16) 78.63.32.23
Librairie Decitre
29, place Bellecour
69002 Lyon   Tel. (16) 72.40.54.54

GERMANY – ALLEMAGNE
OECD Publications and Information Centre
August-Bebel-Allee 6
D-53175 Bonn   Tel. (0228) 959.120
Telefax: (0228) 959.12.17

GREECE – GRÈCE
Librairie Kauffmann
Mavrokordatou 9
106 78 Athens   Tel. (01) 32.55.321
Telefax: (01) 36.33.967

HONG-KONG
Swindon Book Co. Ltd.
13–15 Lock Road
Kowloon, Hong Kong   Tel. 366.80.31
Telefax: 739.49.75

HUNGARY – HONGRIE
Euro Info Service
Margitsziget, Európa Ház
1138 Budapest   Tel. (1) 111.62.16
Telefax : (1) 111.60.61

ICELAND – ISLANDE
Mál Mog Menning
Laugavegi 18, Pósthólf 392
121 Reykjavik   Tel. 162.35.23

INDIA – INDE
Oxford Book and Stationery Co.
Scindia House
New Delhi 110001   Tel.(11) 331.5896/5308
Telefax: (11) 332.5993
17 Park Street
Calcutta 700016   Tel. 240832

INDONESIA – INDONÉSIE
Pdii-Lipi
P.O. Box 269/JKSMG/88
Jakarta 12790   Tel. 583467
Telex: 62 875

IRELAND – IRLANDE
TDC Publishers – Library Suppliers
12 North Frederick Street
Dublin 1   Tel. (01) 874.48.35
Telefax: (01) 874.84.16

ISRAEL
Praedicta
5 Shatner Street
P.O. Box 34030
Jerusalem 91430   Tel. (2) 52.84.90/1/2
Telefax: (2) 52.84.93

ITALY – ITALIE
Libreria Commissionaria Sansoni
Via Duca di Calabria 1/1
50125 Firenze   Tel. (055) 64.54.15
Telefax: (055) 64.12.57
Via Bartolini 29
20155 Milano   Tel. (02) 36.50.83
Editrice e Libreria Herder
Piazza Montecitorio 120
00186 Roma   Tel. 679.46.28
Telefax: 678.47.51
Libreria Hoepli
Via Hoepli 5
20121 Milano   Tel. (02) 86.54.46
Telefax: (02) 805.28.86
Libreria Scientifica
Dott. Lucio de Biasio 'Aeiou'
Via Coronelli, 6
20146 Milano   Tel. (02) 48.95.45.52
Telefax: (02) 48.95.45.48

JAPAN – JAPON
OECD Publications and Information Centre
Landic Akasaka Building
2-3-4 Akasaka, Minato-ku
Tokyo 107   Tel. (81.3) 3586.2016
Telefax: (81.3) 3584.7929

KOREA – CORÉE
Kyobo Book Centre Co. Ltd.
P.O. Box 1658, Kwang Hwa Moon
Seoul   Tel. 730.78.91
Telefax: 735.00.30

MALAYSIA – MALAISIE
Co-operative Bookshop Ltd.
University of Malaya
P.O. Box 1127, Jalan Pantai Baru
59700 Kuala Lumpur
Malaysia   Tel. 756.5000/756.5425
Telefax: 757.3661

MEXICO – MEXIQUE
Revistas y Periodicos Internacionales S.A. de C.V.
Florencia 57 - 1004
Mexico, D.F. 06600   Tel. 207.81.00
Telefax : 208.39.79

NETHERLANDS – PAYS-BAS
SDU Uitgeverij Plantijnstraat
Externe Fondsen
Postbus 20014
2500 EA's-Gravenhage   Tel. (070) 37.89.880
Voor bestellingen: Telefax: (070) 34.75.778

NEW ZEALAND
NOUVELLE-ZÉLANDE
Legislation Services
P.O. Box 12418
Thorndon, Wellington   Tel. (04) 496.5652
Telefax: (04) 496.5698

PRINTED IN FRANCE

•

OECD PUBLICATIONS
2 rue André-Pascal
75775 PARIS CEDEX 16
No. 47425
(10 94 26 1) ISBN 92-64-14218-5
ISSN 0376-6438

•